AN ISLAND GARDEN

AN ISLAND GARDEN

CELIA THAXTER

WITH PICTURES AND ILLUMINATIONS BY
CHILDE HASSAM

Introduction by
Allen Lacy

HOUGHTON MIFFLIN COMPANY
BOSTON
1988

Library of Congress Cataloging-in-Publication Data

Thaxter, Celia Laighton, 1835–1894.
An island garden / by Celia Thaxter ; with pictures and
illuminations by Childe Hassam ; introduction by Allen Lacy.
p.   cm.
ISBN 0-395-48591-6
1. Celia Thaxter's Garden (Appledore Island, Me.) 2. Thaxter,
Celia Laighton, 1835–1894. 3. Gardens — Maine — Appledore Island.
4. Appledore Island (Me.) — Description and travel. I. Title.
[SB466.U7C458 1988]
635.9′09741′95 — dc19   88–20953
                                          CIP

PRINTED IN THE UNITED STATES OF AMERICA

J 10 9 8 7 6 5 4 3 2 1

Publisher's Note

In March 1894, Houghton Mifflin published the first edition — one thousand copies — of *An Island Garden,* the last and best book Celia Thaxter wrote. A second printing of one thousand copies was published in November 1894, a few months after her death, and the book was declared out of print in 1902. Although an edition without illustrations was brought out two years later, this is the first reissue by Houghton Mifflin of the famous Childe Hassam edition.

The paintings commissioned for *An Island Garden* are considered by many to be the most beautiful of Childe Hassam's career and as important to American Impressionism as Monet's paintings of his garden are to French Impressionism.

In the original edition, Hassam's paintings and chapter headings were reproduced by chromolithography, an expensive and painstaking process of color printing in use during the second half of the nineteenth century. The lithographic artist who copied the original work of art may have used as many as thirty stones to make one color reproduction. The chromolithographs for *An Island Garden* were made at Armstrong & Company, which had merged with Houghton Mifflin in 1875. The book's gold-stamped cover, which is reproduced in this edition, was designed by Sarah Wyman Whitman.

Introduction

BY ALLEN LACY

IN THE FOREWORD to *Green Thoughts: A Writer in the Garden*, Eleanor Perènyi makes the claim that "a writer who gardens *is* sooner or later going to write a book about the subject." Celia Thaxter's charming classic, *An Island Garden*, first published in 1894, just a few months before she died at the age of fifty-nine, seems perfectly to exemplify this claim. It illustrates another point, however: Some writers who consider their writing on horticultural topics to play but a minor part in their work would probably be surprised if they knew that their posthumous reputation would rest upon it almost entirely.

So it was with Vita Sackville-West. The lapidary newspaper columns she wrote over a period of many years will be read and savored for decades to come, long after her more ambitious novels and poems have been forgotten. And so it was with Celia Thaxter. Readers who fall under the spell of her lyrical descriptions of the hollyhocks and poppies and scarlet flax in her tiny garden on Appledore, one of the Isles of Shoals off the coast of Portsmouth, New Hampshire, will eagerly want to seek out her poems and other writings. They can only be disappointed. Thaxter considered herself primarily to be a poet, and indeed was taken quite seriously as a poet by such contemporaries as James Russell Lowell, John Greenleaf Whittier, and Sarah Orne Jewett. She earned her reputation as a poet almost instantaneously, with the anonymous publication of her first poem, "Landlocked," in *The Atlantic Monthly* in 1860. But the truth about Celia Thaxter is that her poetry, although competent, was merely that. In *An Island Garden* and also in her correspondence with her family and her friends, however, she stands out as one of America's masters of English prose.

There is nothing particularly surprising about this fact. Mrs. Thaxter was a highly popular poet, and highly popular poets, who speak to and for the people of their own day, writing on the themes and topics that interest them and saying the things that they expect to be said, often have little to say to readers a century later. They deal in conventional sentiments that also pass with time. Such poetry came easily to Celia Thaxter, but prose gave her more trouble. Encouraged in 1862 by James T. Fields, the editor of *The Atlantic Monthly*, to write prose as well as poetry for him, she asked for his patience, citing the harshness of her circumstances as a wife and mother. "Meanwhile," she wrote, "here are some verses which have evolved among the pots and kettles, to which you're welcome, if they're good enough for you. Verses can grow where prose can't." Throughout her writing career (a career pursued in the few spare moments she had from housework during most of the year in her own home and during the summer at the resort hotel her family owned

on Appledore), she favored verse and complained about
her difficulties with prose. In one letter to her close friend
Sarah Orne Jewett in 1893, she expressed doubts about
the manuscript of *An Island Garden*: "I have been doing
this work without a particle of enthusiasm, in a most per-
functory manner."

But writers are notoriously their own least perceptive
critics. When Thaxter wrote poetry about plants, as in
the poem called "My Garden," her easy rhymes did not
allow her to call on her obviously keen powers of observation. The poem addresses both the reader and its subject
in mere generalities:

> It blossomed by the summer sea,
>   A tiny space of tangled bloom
> Wherein so many flowers found room
>   A miracle it seemed to be!
>   .   .   .   .
> More dear to me than words can tell
>   Was every cup and spray and leaf,
> Too perfect for a life so brief
>   Seemed every star and bud and bell.

An Island Garden, however, deals precisely with the
extremely specific and particular events that took place in
Thaxter's garden on Appledore. She talks about sowing
seeds that are difficult to transplant in eggshells — an
ingenious idea, and apparently a successful one. She
writes about weeding with the sure knowledge of someone
who has weeded for many years and who knows that the
task will never end. In exacting detail her book follows

the progress of the seasons in a gardener's year and the
succession of colors and scents from the first wallflowers
of spring through the last wild roses of autumn. And it
treats each plant in all of its individuality of character, as
looked at with a hand lens. Here, almost at random, is a
passage that, after sounding the same conventional note
as in "My Garden" about feelings "more than words can
tell," presents some very telling words about the eschscholtzia, or California poppy:

> As I hold the flower in my hand and think of trying to de-
> scribe it, I realize how poor a creature I am, how impotent
> are words in the presence of such perfection. It is held up-
> right upon a straight and polished stem, its petals curving
> upward and outward into the cup of light, pure gold with a
> lustrous satin sheen; a rich orange is painted on the gold,
> drawn in infinitely fine lines to a point in the centre of
> the edge of each petal, so that the effect is that of a di-
> amond of flame in a cup of gold. It is not enough that the
> powdery anthers are orange bordered with gold; they are
> whirled about the very heart of the flower like a revolving
> Catharine-wheel of fire. In the centre of the anthers is a
> shining point of warm sea-green, a last, consummate touch
> which makes the beauty of the blossom supreme.

Celia Thaxter's place in the history of American writing on gardening is clear.

The first American book on gardening worthy of the
name was Bernard McMahon's *The American Gardener's
Calendar* (1806), which initiated almost a century of
purely practical horticultural literature, dispensing advice
about what to do and when to do it and dealing primarily

with the useful plants of the orchard and the kitchen garden. A few writers, such as the enormously influential
Andrew Jackson Downing, raised their voices on ques-
tions of social policy, notably the need to establish public
parks in America's rapidly growing industrial cities.
Nineteenth-century garden writing was often moralistic
and more than faintly tinctured with asceticism. The
growing of ornamental flowers was justified for theo-
logical reasons: They were God's parables for human-
kind, the lilies of the field mentioned in the Sermon on the
Mount.

None of these things had very much to do with Celia
Thaxter. Her poetry was conventionally religious (although her letters create doubt about her real views).
An Island Garden occasionally reverts to the traditional
horticultural theology, as when she speaks of finding
among her poppies "the exhaustless power of the great
Inventor." But at base Thaxter's appreciation of gardening was purely aesthetic. She loved flowers entirely for
their own sake and for the sake of the pleasure they gave
her. She gave wholehearted recognition to the pleasures
of the senses as good in themselves. It is no accident that
leading American musicians and painters, notably including Childe Hassam, the Impressionist, congregated on
Appledore every summer during her final years, when
the living room of her cottage with its hop-covered veranda and its little garden out front was a true salon in
the Parisian sense.

Although she wrote only one book on gardening, Celia
Thaxter's influence has been strong. Even if much Amer-

ican garden writing in the twentieth century has treated
this country as a horticultural colony of Great Britain,
where all the great garden writers are sometimes thought
to dwell, many of our best writers have treasured Thaxter's work and learned from it. It initiates a noble line of
horticultural writing that includes such figures as Alice
Morse Earle, Louise Beebe Wilder, and Elizabeth Law-
rence, who often spoke to her friends about the fondness
she felt for this slender volume of winsome prose about
the joys and also the frustrations a garden brings. It will
continue to find and delight new readers, especially now
that it is available from its original publisher in a fac-
simile of the first edition, with reproductions of all the
chromolithographs made from Childe Hassam's water-
color paintings of the Thaxter garden.

The reissue of this book naturally raises curiosity about
its author and her life, since Celia Thaxter is today hardly
a household name, as she was in nineteenth-century literary circles. The story has been told, and told most pleasantly and completely, in a biography, *Sandpiper: The Life
and Times of Celia Thaxter*, written by Thaxter's grand-
daughter, Rosamond Thaxter.

In brief, Thaxter was born in Portsmouth, New Hampshire, in 1835. At the age of four she moved to tiny White
Island, one of the Isles of Shoals, where her father,
Thomas B. Laighton, was a lighthouse keeper. Her earliest education and that of her two brothers was at his
hands. In 1848 the family moved to nearby Hog Island,
which her father had bought and renamed Appledore.

Here the Laightons built a summer resort hotel, whose guests during the second half of the nineteenth century included many leading figures in New England's literary and cultural aristocracy.

In time Celia's education was handed over to a tutor, a young Harvard graduate named Levi Thaxter, who asked for her hand in marriage when she was only fifteen. Her father at first refused, but the following year the couple married, and Levi took his bride from the isles where she had grown up to the hills of Massachusetts. Three children followed, but their parents led rather separate lives, especially following Levi Thaxter's near-drowning in a sudden fall storm off Appledore in 1855. This incident left him unwilling to return to the island again, thus bringing about prolonged separation from Celia during the summer months, when she helped her parents and her brothers run their hotel. Mr. Thaxter, who tried several occupations, seems never to have found one that fit, except for giving public readings of the poetry of Robert Browning. He died in 1884, ten years before his wife.

A sad thing about gardens is that they often do not survive their gardeners, or they don't survive them very long. And thus it was with Celia Thaxter's island garden. Relatives kept it up for a while, and visitors came regularly in the summer to see her parlor, with its grand piano, its wall covered with paintings by Childe Hassam and other friends, and its many vases filled with flowers picked each morning from the garden. But the hotel and many other buildings on Appledore, including Thaxter's cottage, burned to the ground in 1914. The island fell on bad times. The U.S. Navy used it for many years as a target range for cannon fire. Huge colonies of sea gulls, fairly rare there in the nineteenth century, took the place over as a rookery. Poison ivy and scrubby vegetation such as alders began to invade. Thaxter's garden lived on only in the pages of her book — and in Hassam's paintings.

But the story of this fabled garden has a happy ending. There is now an outpost of Cornell University on Appledore, and its director in 1978, Professor John Kingsbury, undertook to restore the garden Celia Thaxter had made, using the plans in her book. Today the garden is lovingly tended from early spring until late fall by Virginia Chisholm of Rye Beach, New Hampshire. There is regular boat service from Portsmouth to Star Island, where the Star Island Corporation, a religious group, maintains a summer hotel for conferences. On request, the marine station will fetch visitors from Star Island in a whaleboat and make the choppy crossing to Appledore. Here, in a cleared area in front of the old foundations of Celia Thaxter's summer cottage, stands the replica of her garden, bright and beautiful with the same flowers she planted and celebrated in *An Island Garden*.

AN ISLAND GARDEN
BY CELIA THAXTER

WITH PAINTINGS BY
CHILDE HASSAM

AN ISLAND GARDEN

BY CELIA THAXTER
WITH PICTURES AND
ILLUMINATIONS BY
CHILDE HASSAM

BOSTON AND NEW YORK
HOUGHTON MIFFLIN & CO.
The Riverside Press, Cambridge
MDCCCXCV

The Riverside Press, Cambridge, Mass., U. S. A.
Electrotyped and Printed by H. O. Houghton & Company.

TO

MRS. MARY HEMENWAY

"WHOSE LARGENESS OF HEART IS EVEN AS THE

SAND ON THE SEASHORE"

THIS VOLUME

IS AFFECTIONATELY INSCRIBED

T the Isles of Shoals, among the ledges of the largest island, Appledore, lies the small garden which in the following pages I have endeavored to describe. Ever since I could remember anything, flowers have been like dear friends to me, comforters, inspirers, powers to uplift and to cheer. A lonely child, living on the lighthouse island ten miles away from the mainland, every blade of grass that sprang out of the ground, every humblest weed, was precious in my sight, and I began a little garden when not more than five years old. From this, year after year, the larger one, which has given so much pleasure to so many people, has grown. The first small bed at the lighthouse island contained only Marigolds, pot Marigolds, fire-colored blossoms which were the joy of my heart and the delight of my eyes. This scrap of garden, literally not more than a

yard square, with its barbaric splendors of color,
I worshiped like any Parsee. When I planted
the dry, brown seeds I noticed how they were
shaped, like crescents, with a fine line of ornamental dots, a " beading " along the whole length
of the centre, — from this crescent sprang the
Marigold plant, each of whose flowers was like

> " a mimic sun,
> With ray-like florets round a disk-like face."

In my childish mind I pondered much on this
fact of the crescent growing into the full-rayed
orb. Many thoughts had I of all the flowers I
knew; very dear were they, so that after I had
gathered them I felt sorry, and I had a safe place
between the rocks to which I carried them when
they were withered, and hid them away from all
eyes, they were so precious even then.

The dear flowers! Summer after summer they
return to me, always young and fresh and beautiful; but so many of the friends who have watched
them and loved them with me are gone, and they
return no more. I think of the lament of Mos-
chus for Bion : —

" Ah me, when the Mallows wither in the garden, and the green Parsley, and the curled tendrils of the Anise, on a later day they spring, in
another year; but we men, we, the great and
mighty, or wise, when once we have died, in hollow earth we sleep, gone down into silence."

Into silence! How deep, how unbroken is that silence! But because of tender memories of loving eyes that see them no more, my flowers are yet more beloved and tenderly cherished.

Year after year the island garden has grown in beauty and charm, so that in response to the many entreaties of strangers as well as friends who have said to me, summer after summer, " Tell us how you do it! Write a book about it and tell us how it is done, that we may go also and do likewise," I have written this book at last. Truly it contains the fruit of much sweet and bitter experience. Of what I speak I know, and of what I know I have freely given. I trust it may help the patient gardener to a reasonable measure of success, and to that end I have spared no smallest detail that seemed to me necessary, no suggestion that might prove helpful.

DUST.

Here is a problem, a wonder for all to see.
   Look at this marvelous thing I hold in my hand!
This is a magic surprising, a mystery
   Strange as a miracle, harder to understand.

What is it? Only a handful of earth: to your touch
   A dry rough powder you trample beneath your feet,
Dark and lifeless; but think for a moment, how much
   It hides and holds that is beautiful, bitter, or sweet.

Think of the glory of color! The red of the rose,
   Green of the myriad leaves and the fields of grass,
Yellow as bright as the sun where the daffodil blows,
   Purple where violets nod as the breezes pass.

Think of the manifold form, of the oak and the vine,
   Nut, and fruit, and cluster, and ears of corn;
Of the anchored water-lily, a thing divine,
   Unfolding its dazzling snow to the kiss of morn.

Think of the delicate perfumes borne on the gale,
   Of the golden willow catkin's odor of spring,
Of the breath of the rich narcissus waxen-pale,
   Of the sweet pea's flight of flowers, of the nettle's sting.

Strange that this lifeless thing gives vine, flower, tree,
   Color and shape and character, fragrance too;
That the timber that builds the house, the ship for the sea,
   Out of this powder its strength and its toughness drew!

That the cocoa among the palms should suck its milk
   From this dry dust, while dates from the self-same soil
Summon their sweet rich fruit: that our shining silk
   The mulberry leaves should yield to the worm's slow toil.

How should the poppy steal sleep from the very source
   That grants to the grapevine juice that can madden or
     cheer?
How does the weed find food for its fabric coarse
   Where the lilies proud their blossoms pure uprear?

Who shall compass or fathom God's thought profound?
   We can but praise, for we may not understand;
But there's no more beautiful riddle the whole world round
   Than is hid in this heap of dust I hold in my hand.

THE LIST OF PICTURES FOR AN
ISLAND GARDEN

AN ISLAND GARDEN
BY CELIA THAXTER

WITH PAINTINGS BY
CHILDE HASSAM

PLAN OF GARDEN WITH LIST OF FLOWERS

1 Akebia Quinata
2 Asa Gray Nasturtiums
3 Asters
4 Asters and Lavatera
5 Bachelors' Buttons
6 Bride Poppies
7 Clematis, white
8 Clematis, blue
9 Cleome Pungens
10 Columbine
11 Coreopsis Coronata and Corn-
     flowers
12 Coreopsis Lanceolata
13 Crimson Phlox
14 Damask Rose

15 Echinocystis Lobata
16 Foxgloves
17 Golden Banner Corcopsis
18 Helianthus
19 Hollyhocks
20 Honeysuckles
21 Hop
22 Hugelia
23 Iceland Poppies
24 Jacqueminot, Damask, and La
     France Roses
25 Japan Honeysuckles
26 Japan Hop
27 Larkspur
28 Lavender

29 Lilies
30 Love-in-a-Mist
31 Margaret Pinks
32 Mangolds
33 Mignonette
34 Oriental Poppy
35 Peonies
36 Picotee Pinks
37 Poppies
38 Rose-colored Iceland Poppies
39 Rose Campion
40 Scotch Roses
41 Shirley Poppies
42 Single Dahlias
43 Snowdrops, etc.

44 Sweet Peas
45 Sweet Rocket
46 Sweet William
47 Sunflowers
48 Tall Phlox
49 Tea Roses
50 Travelers' Joy
51 Verbenas
52 Vines
53 Violets
54 Wallflowers
55 Water Lilies
56 White Lilies
57 Wistaria

NOTE. — The garden is 50 ft. long by 15 ft. wide, and is surrounded by a border of all sorts of mixed flowers. A bank of flowers at the southwest corner slopes from the garden fence.

OF all the wonderful things in the wonderful universe of God, nothing seems to me more surprising than the planting of a seed in the blank earth and the result thereof. Take a Poppy seed, for instance: it lies in your palm, the merest atom of matter, hardly visible, a speck, a pin's point in bulk, but within it is imprisoned a spirit of beauty ineffable, which will break its bonds and emerge from the dark ground and blossom in a splendor so dazzling as to baffle all powers of description.

The Genie in the Arabian tale is not half so astonishing. In this tiny casket lie folded roots, stalks, leaves, buds, flowers, seed-vessels, — surpassing color and beautiful form, all that goes to make up a plant which is as gigantic in proportion to the bounds that confine it as the Oak is to the acorn. You may watch this marvel from beginning to end in a few weeks' time, and if you realize how great a marvel it is, you can but be

3

lost in " wonder, love, and praise."   All seeds are
most interesting, whether winged like the Dandelion and Thistle, to fly on every breeze afar; or
barbed to catch in the wool of cattle or the gar-
ments of men, to be borne away and spread in all
directions over the land; or feathered like the
little polished silvery shuttlecocks of the Corn-
flower, to whirl in the wind abroad and settle
presently, point downward, into the hospitable
ground; or oared like the Maple, to row out
upon the viewless tides of the air.   But if I were
to pause on the threshold of the year to consider
the miracles of seeds alone, I should never, I fear,
reach my garden plot at all!

He who is born with a silver spoon in his
mouth is generally considered a fortunate person,
but his good fortune is small compared to that of
the happy mortal who enters this world with a
passion for flowers in his soul.   I use the word
advisedly, though it seems a weighty one for the
subject, for I do not mean a light or shallow affec-
tion, or even an æsthetic admiration; no butterfly
interest, but a real love which is worthy of the
name, which is capable of the dignity of sacrifice,
great enough to bear discomfort of body and dis-
appointment of spirit, strong enough to fight a
thousand enemies for the thing beloved, with
power, with judgment, with endless patience, and
to give with everything else a subtler stimulus
which is more delicate and perhaps more necessary than all the rest.

Often I hear people say, " How do you make
your plants flourish like this?" as they admire

the little flower patch I cultivate in summer, or the window gardens that bloom for me in the winter; " I can never make my plants blossom like this! What is your secret?" And I answer with one word, " Love." For that includes all, — the patience that endures continual trial, the constancy that makes perseverance possible, the power of foregoing ease of mind and body to minister to the necessities of the thing beloved, and the subtle bond of sympathy which is as important, if not more so, than all the rest. For though I cannot go so far as a witty friend of mine, who says that when he goes out to sit in the shade on his piazza, his Wistaria vine leans toward him and lays her head on his shoulder, I am fully and intensely aware that plants are conscious of love and respond to it as they do to nothing else. You may give them all they need of food and drink and make the conditions of their existence as favorable as possible, and they may grow and bloom, but there is a certain ineffable something that will be missing if you do not love them, a delicate glory too spiritual to be caught and put into words. The Norwegians have a pretty and significant word, " Opelske," which they use in speaking of the care of flowers. It means literally " loving up," or cherishing them into health and vigor.

Like the musician, the painter, the poet, and the rest, the true lover of flowers is born, not made. And he is born to happiness in this vale of tears, to a certain amount of the purest joy that earth can give her children, joy that is tranquil,

innocent, uplifting, unfailing. Given a little patch
of ground, with time to take care of it, with tools
to work it and seeds to plant in it, he has all he
needs, and Nature with her dews and suns and
showers and sweet airs gives him her aid. But
he soon learns that it is not only liberty of which
eternal vigilance is the price; the saying applies
quite as truly to the culture of flowers, for the
name of their enemies is legion, and they must
be fought early and late, day and night, without
cessation. The cutworm, the wire-worm, the
pansy-worm, the thrip, the rose-beetle, the aphis,
the mildew, and many more, but worst of all the
loathsome slug, a slimy, shapeless creature that
devours every fair and exquisite thing in the garden, — the flower lover must seek all these with
unflagging energy, and if possible exterminate
the whole. So only may he and his precious
flowers purchase peace. Manifold are the means
of destruction to be employed, for almost every
pest requires a different poison. On a closet
shelf which I keep especially for them are rows
of tin pepper- boxes, each containing a deadly
powder, all carefully labeled. For the thrip that
eats out the leaves of the Rosebush till they are
nothing but fibrous skeletons of woody lace, there
is hellebore, to be shaken on the under side of all
the leaves, — mark you, the *under* side, and think of
the difficulties involved in the process of so treat-
ing hundreds of leaves! For the blue or gray
mildew and the orange mildew another box holds
powdered sulphur, — this is more easily applied,
shaken over the tops of the bushes, but all the

leaves must be reached, none neglected at your peril! Still another box contains yellow snuff for the green aphis, but he is almost impossible to manage, — let once his legions get a foothold, good-by to any hope for you! Lime, salt, paris green, cayenne pepper, kerosene emulsion, whale-oil soap, the list of weapons is long indeed, with which one must fight the garden's foes! And it must be done with such judgment, persistence, patience, accuracy, and watchful care! It seems to me the worst of all the plagues is the slug, the snail without a shell. He is beyond description repulsive, a mass of sooty, shapeless slime, and he devours everything. He seems to thrive on all the poisons known; salt and lime are the only things that have power upon him, at least the only things I have been able to find so far. But salt and lime must be used very carefully, or they destroy the plant as effectually as the slug would do. Every night, while the season is yet young, and the precious growths just beginning to make their way upward, feeling their strength, I go at sunset and heap along the edge of the flower beds air-slaked lime, or round certain most valuable plants a ring of the same, — the slug cannot cross this while it is fresh, but should it be left a day or two it loses its strength, it has no more power to burn, and the enemy may slide over it unharmed, leaving his track of slime. On many a solemn midnight have I stolen from my bed to visit my cherished treasures by the pale glimpses of the moon, that I might be quite sure the protecting rings were still strong enough to save them, for the slug eats by night, he is invisible by day unless it rains or the sky be overcast. He hides under every damp board or in any nook of shade, because the sun is death to him. I use salt for his destruction in the same way as the lime, but it is so dangerous for the plants, I am always afraid of it. Neither of these things must be left about them when they are watered lest the lime or salt sink into the earth in such quantities as to injure the tender roots. I have little cages of fine wire netting which I adjust over some plants, carefully heaping the earth about them to leave no loophole through which the enemy may crawl, and round some of the beds, which are inclosed in strips of wood, boxed, to hold the earth in place, long shallow troughs of wood are nailed and filled with salt to keep off the pests. Nothing that human ingenuity can suggest do I leave untried to save my beloved flowers! Every evening at sunset I pile lime and salt about my pets, and every morning remove it before I sprinkle them at sunrise. The salt dissolves of itself in the humid sea air and in the dew, so around those for whose safety I am most solicitous I lay rings of pasteboard on which to heap it, to be certain of doing the plants no harm. Judge, reader, whether all this requires strength, patience, perseverance, hope! It is hard work beyond a doubt, but I do not grudge it, for great is my reward. Before I knew what to do to save my garden from the slugs, I have stood at evening rejoicing over rows of fresh emerald leaves just springing in rich lines along the beds, and woke in the morning to find the whole space stripped of any sign of green, as blank as a board over which a carpenter's plane has passed.

In the thickest of my fight with the slugs some one said to me, "Everything living has its enemy; the enemy of the slug is the toad. Why don't you import toads?"

I snatched at the hope held out to me, and immediately wrote to a friend on the continent, "In the name of the Prophet, Toads!" At once a force of only too willing boys was set about the work of catching every toad within reach, and one day in June a boat brought a box to me from the far-off express office. A piece of wire netting was nailed across the top, and upon the earth with which it was half filled, reposing among some dry and dusty green leaves, sat three dry and dusty toads, wearily gazing at nothing. Is this all, I thought, only three! Hardly worth sending so far. Poor creatures, they looked so arid and wilted, I took up the hose and turned upon them a gentle shower of fresh cool water, flooding the box. I was not prepared for the result! The dry, baked earth heaved tumultuously; up came dusky heads and shoulders and bright eyes by the dozen. A sudden concert of liquid sweet notes was poured out on the air from the whole rejoicing company. It was really beautiful to hear that musical ripple of delight. I surveyed them with eager interest as they sat singing and blinking together. "You are not handsome," I said, as I took a hammer and wrenched off the wire cover that shut them in, "but you will be lovely in my sight if you will help me to destroy mine enemy;" and with that I turned the box on its side and out they skipped into a perfect paradise of food and shade. All summer I came upon them in different parts of the garden, waxing fatter and fatter till they were as round as apples. In the autumn baby toads no larger than my thumb nail were found hopping merrily over the whole island. There were sixty in that first importation; next summer I received ninety more. But alas! small dogs discover them in the grass and delight to tear and worry them to death, and the rats prey upon them so that many perish in that way; yet I hope to keep enough to preserve my garden in spite of fate.

In France the sale of toads for the protection of gardens is universal, and I find under the head of "A Garden Friend," in a current newspaper, the following item: —

"One is amused, in walking through the great Covent Garden Market, London, to find toads among the commodities offered for sale. In such favor do these familiar reptiles stand with English market gardeners that they readily command a shilling apiece. . . . The toad has indeed no superior as a destroyer of noxious insects, and as he possesses no bad habits and is entirely inoffensive himself, every owner of a garden should treat him with the utmost hospitality. It is quite worth the while not only to offer any simple inducements which suggest themselves for rendering the premises attractive to him, but should he show a tendency to wander away from them, to

go so far as to exercise a gentle force in bringing him back to the regions where his services may be of the greatest utility."

One of the most universal pests is the cut-worm, a fat, naked worm of varying lengths. I have seen them two inches and a half long and as large round as my little finger. This unpleasant creature lives in the ground about the roots of plants. I have known one to go through a whole row of Sweet Peas and cut them off smoothly above the roots just as a sickle would do; there lay the dead stalks in melancholy line. It makes no difference what the plant may be, they will level all without distinction. The only remedy for this plague is to scratch all about in the earth round the roots of the plants where their ravages begin, dig the worms out, and kill them. I have found sometimes whole nests of them with twenty young ones at once. Lime dug into the soil is recommended to destroy them, but there is no remedy so sure as seeking a personal interview and slaying them on the spot. They are not by any means always to be discovered, but the gardener must again exercise that endless patience upon which the success of the garden depends, and be never weary of seeking them till they are found.

Another enemy to my flowers, and a truly formidable one, is my little friend the song-sparrow. Literally he gives the plot of ground no peace if I venture to put seeds into it. He obliges me to start almost all my seeds in boxes, to be trans-planted into the beds when the plants are suf-

ficiently tough to have lost their delicacy for his
palate and are no longer adapted to his ideal of
a salad.   All the Sweet Peas, many hundreds of
the delicate plants, are every one grown in this
way.   When they are a foot high with roots a
foot long they are all transplanted separately.
Even then the little robber attacks them, and,
though he cannot uproot, he will "yank" and
twist the stems till he has murdered them in the
vain hope of pulling up the remnant of a pea
which he judges to be somewhere beneath the
surface.   Then must sticks and supports be
draped with yards of old fishing nets to protect
the unfortunates, and over the Mignonette, and
even the Poppy beds and others, I must lay a
cover of closely woven wire to keep out the
marauder.   But I love him still, though sadly he
torments me.   I have adored his fresh music ever
since I was a child, and I only laugh as he sits
on the fence watching me with his bright black
eyes; there is something quaintly comical and
delightful about him, and he sings like a friendly
angel.   From him I can protect myself, but I
cannot save my garden so easily from the hideous
slug, for which I have no sentiment save only a
fury of extermination.

If possible, it is much the best way to begin in
the autumn to work for the garden of the next
spring, and the first necessity is the preparation
of the soil.   If the gardener is as fortunate as I
am at the Isles of Shoals, there will be no trouble
in doing this, for there the barn manure is heaped
in certain waste places, out of the way, and left

till every change of wind and weather, of temperature and climate, have so wrought upon it that
it becomes a fine, odorless, velvet-brown earth,
rich in all needful sustenance for almost all
plants, — "well-rotted manure," the "Old Farmer's Almanac" calls it.   But if there is no mine
of wealth such as this from which to draw, there
are many fertilizers, sold by all seed and plant
merchants, which will answer the purpose very
well.   I have, however, never found anything to
equal barn manure as food for flowers, and if not
possible to obtain this in a state fit for immediate
use, it is best to have several cart-loads taken
from the barn in autumn and piled in a heap near
the garden plot, there to remain all winter, till
rains and snows and cold and heat, all the powers
of the elements, have worked their will upon it,
and rendered it fit for use in the coming spring.
Many people make a compost heap, — it is an
excellent thing to do, — piling turf and dead
leaves and refuse together, and leaving it to slow
decay till it becomes a fine, rich, mellow earth.
In my case the barn manure has been more easily
obtained, and so I have used it always and with
complete success, but I have a compost heap also,
to use for plants which do not like barn manure.

As late as possible, before the ground freezes,
I dig up the single Dahlia tubers (there are no
double ones in my garden), and put them in
boxes filled with clean, dry sand, to keep in a
frost-free cellar till spring. I find Gladiolus bulbs,
Tulips, Lilies, and so forth, will keep perfectly well
in the ground through the winter at the Shoals.

Over the Foxgloves, Iceland Poppies, Wallflowers, Mullein Pinks, Picotees, and other perennials, I scatter the fine barn manure lightly, over the Hollyhocks more heavily, and about the Rose-bushes I heap it up high, quite two thirds of their whole height, — you cannot give them too much, only be careful that enough of their length, that is to say, one third of the highest sprays, are left out in the air, that they may breathe. In the spring this manure must all be carefully dug into the ground round their roots. About Honey-suckles, Clematis, Grapevine, and so forth, I pile it plentifully, mixed with wood ashes, which is espe-cially good for Grapevine and Rosebushes. But the white Lilies, and indeed Lilies generally, do not like to come in contact with the barn manure, so they are protected by leaves and boughs, and the earth near them enriched in the spring, care-fully avoiding the contact which they dislike. When putting the garden in order in the autumn, all the dry Sweet Pea vines, and dead stalks of all kinds, which are pulled up to clear the ground, I heap for shelter over the perennials, being careful to lay small bayberry branches over first, so that I may in no way interfere with a free circulation of air about them. In open spaces where no perennials are growing I scatter the manure thickly, that the ground may be slowly and surely enriched all through the winter and be ready to furnish bountiful nourishment for every green growing thing through the summer. When the little plot is spaded in April, all this is dug in and mixed thoroughly with the soil.

When the snow is still blowing against the
window-pane in January and February, and the
wild winds are howling without, what pleasure it
is to plan for summer that is to be! Small shallow wooden boxes are ready, filled with mellow
earth (of which I am always careful to lay in a
supply before the ground freezes in the autumn),
sifted and made damp; into it the precious seeds
are dropped with a loving hand. The Pansy
seeds lie like grains of gold on the dark soil. I
think as I look at them of the splendors of impe-
rial purples folded within them, of their gold and
blue and bronze, of all the myriad combinations
of superb color in their rich velvets. Each one of
these small golden grains means such a wealth
of beauty and delight! Then the thin flake-like
brown seeds of the annual Stocks or Gillyflowers;
one little square of paper holds the white Princess
Alice variety, so many thick double spikes of
fragrant snow lie hidden in each thin dry flake!
Another paper holds the pale rose-color, another
the delicate lilacs, or deep purples, or shrimp
pinks, or vivid crimsons, — all are dropped on the
earth, lightly covered, gently pressed down; then
sprinkled and set in a warm place, they are left to
germinate. Next I come to the single Dahlia
seeds, rough, dry, misshapen husks, that, being
planted thus early, will blossom by the last of
June, unfolding their large rich stars in great
abundance till frost. They blossom in every
variety of color except blue; all shades of red
from faint rose to black maroon, and all are gold-
centred. They are every shade of yellow from

sulphur to flame, — king's flowers, I call them,
stately and splendid.

All these and many more are planted.   For
those that do not bear transplanting I prepare
other quarters, half filling shallow boxes with
sand, into which I set rows of egg-shells close
together, each shell cut off at one end, with a
hole for drainage at the bottom.   These are filled
with earth, and in them the seeds of the lovely
yellow, white, and orange Iceland Poppies are
sowed.   By and by, when comes the happy time
for setting them out in the garden beds, the shell
can be broken away from the oval ball of earth that
holds their roots without disturbing them, and
they are transplanted almost without knowing it.
It is curious how differently certain plants feel
about this matter of transplanting.   The more
you move a Pansy about the better it seems to
like it, and many annuals grow all the better for
one transplanting; but to a Poppy it means death,
unless it is done in some such careful way as I
have described.

The boxes of seeds are put in a warm, dark
place, for they only require heat and moisture till
they germinate.   Then when the first precious
green leaves begin to appear, what a pleasure it
is to wait and tend on the young growths, which
are moved carefully to some cool, sunny chamber
window in a room where no fire is kept, for heat
becomes the worst enemy at this stage, and they
spindle and dwindle if not protected from it.
When they are large enough, having attained to
their second leaves, each must be put into a little

pot or egg-shell by itself (all except the Poppies and their companions, already in egg-shells), so that by the time the weather is warm enough they will be ready to be set out, stout and strong, for early blooming.

This pleasant business goes on during the winter in the picturesque old town of Portsmouth, New Hampshire, whither I repair in the autumn from the Isles of Shoals, remaining through the cold weather and returning to the islands on the first of April. My upper windows all winter are filled with young Wallflowers, Stocks, single Dahlias, Hollyhocks, Poppies, and many other garden plants, which are watched and tended with the most faithful care till the time comes for transporting them over the seas to Appledore. A small steam tug, the Pinafore, carries me and my household belongings over to the islands, and a pretty sight is the little vessel when she starts out from the old brown wharves and steams away down the beautiful Piscataqua River, with her hurricane deck awave with green leaves and flowers, for all the world like a May Day procession. My blossoming house plants go also, and there are Palms and Ferns and many other lovely things that make the small boat gay indeed. All the boxes of sprouted seedlings are carefully packed in wide square baskets to keep them steady, and the stout young plants hold up their strong stems and healthy green leaves, and take the wind and sun bravely as the vessel goes tossing over the salt waves out to sea.

By the first of April it is time to plant Sweet

Peas. From this time till the second week in
May, when one may venture to transplant into
the garden, the boxes containing the myriads of
seedlings must be carefully watched and tended,
put out of doors on piazza roofs and balcony
through the days and taken in again at night,
solicitously protected from too hot suns and too
rough winds, too heavy rains or too low a temperature, — they require continual care. But it is
joy to give them all they need, and pleasure indeed to watch their vigorous growth. Meanwhile
there is much delightful work to be done in making the small garden plot ready. This little island
garden of mine is so small that the amount of
pure delight it gives in the course of a summer
is something hardly to be credited. It lies along
the edge of a piazza forty or fifty feet long, sloping to the south, not more than fifteen feet wide,
sheltered from the north winds and open to the
sun. The whole piazza is thickly draped with
vines, Hops, Honeysuckles, blue and white Clematis, Cinnamon Vine, *Mina Lobata*, Wistaria,
Nasturtiums, Morning - glories, Japanese Hops,
Woodbine, and the beautiful and picturesque
Wild Cucumber (*Echinocystus Lobata*), which in
July nearly smothers everything else and clothes
itself in a veil of filmy white flowers in loose clusters, fragrant, but never too sweet, always refreshing and exquisite. The vines make a grateful
green shade, doubly delightful for that there are
no trees on my island, and the shade is most welcome in the wide brilliancy of sea and sky.

In the first week of April the ground is spaded

for me; after that no hands touch it save my own throughout the whole season. Day after day it is so pleasant working in the bright cool spring air, for as yet the New England spring is alert and brisk in temperature and shows very little softening in its moods. But by the seventh day of the month, as I stand pruning the Rosebushes, there is a flutter of glad wings, and lo! the first house martins! Beautiful creatures, with their white breasts and steel-blue wings, wheeling, chattering, and scolding at me, for they think I stand too near their little brown house on the corner of the piazza eaves, and they let me know their opinion by coming as near as they dare and snapping their beaks at me with a low guttural sound of displeasure. But after a few days, when they have found they cannot scare me and that I do not interfere with them, they conclude that I am a harmless kind of creature and endure me with tranquillity. Straightway they take possession of their summer quarters and begin to build their cosy nest within. Oh, then the weeks of joyful work, the love-making, the cooing, chattering, calling, in tones of the purest delight and content, the tilting against the wind on burnished wings, the wheeling, fluttering, coquetting, and caressing, the while they bring feathers and straw and shreds and down for their nest-weaving, — all this goes on till after the eggs are laid, when they settle down into comparative quiet. Then often the father bird sits and meditates happily in the sun upon his tiny brown chimney-top, while the mother bird broods below. Or they

go out and take a dip in the air together, or sit
conversing in pretty cadences a little space, till
mother bird must hie indoors to the eggs she
dare not leave longer lest they grow chill.   And
this sweet little drama is repeated all about the
island, on sunny roofs and corners and tall posts,
wherever a bird house has been built for their
convenience.   All through April and May I
watch them as I go to and fro about my business,
while they attend to theirs; we do not interfere
with each other; they have made up their minds
to endure me, but I adore them!   Flattered indeed am I if, while I am at work upon the flower
beds below, father martin comes and sits close to
me on the fence rail and chatters musically, unmindful of my quiet movements, quite fearless
and at home.

While I am busy with pleasant preparation
and larger hope, I rejoice in the beauty of the
pure white Snowdrops I found blossoming in their
sunny corner when I arrived on the first of April,
fragile winged things with their delicate sea-green
markings and fresh, grass-like leaves.   Ever since
the first of March have they been blossoming,
and the Crocus flowers begin, as if blown out of
the earth, like long, lovely bubbles of gold and
purple, or white, pure or streaked with lilac, to
break, under the noon sun, into beautiful petals,
showing the orange anthers like flame within.
And the little Scilla Siberica hangs its enchanting bells out to the breeze, blue, oh, blue as the
deep sea water at its bluest under cloudless skies.
And later, yellow Daffodils and Jonquils, "Tulips

dashed with fiery dew," the exquisite, mystic poet's Narcissus, and one crimson Peony, — my little garden has not room for more than one of these large plants, so early blossoming and at their end so soon.

In the first week of May every year punctually arrive the barn swallows and the sandpipers at the Isles of Shoals. This seems a very common-place statement of a very simple fact, but would it were possible to convey in words the sense of delight with which they are welcomed on this sea-surrounded rock!

Some morning in the first of May I sit in the sunshine and soft air, transplanting my young Pansies and Gillyflowers into the garden beds, — father and mother martin on the fence watching me and talking to each other in a charming language, the import of which is clear enough, though my senses are not sufficiently delicate to comprehend the words. The song-sparrows pour out their simple, friendly lays from bush and wall and fence and gable peak all about me. Down in a hollow I hear the brimming note of the white-throated sparrow, — brimming is the only word that expresses it, — like "a beaker full of the warm South," — such joy, such overflowing measure of bliss! There is a challenge from a robin, perhaps, or a bobolink sends down his "brook o' laughter through the air," or high and far a curlew calls; there is a gentle lapping of waves from the full tide, for the sea is only a stone's-throw from my garden fence. I hear the voices of the children prattling not far away; there are no other sounds. Suddenly from the shore comes a clear cry thrice repeated, " Sweet, sweet, sweet !" And I call to my neighbor, my brother, working also in his garden plot, " The sandpiper ! Do you hear him ? " and the glad news goes from mouth to mouth, " The sandpiper has come !" Oh, the lovely note again and again repeated, " Sweet, sweet, sweet !" echoing softly in the stillness of the tide-brimmed coves, where the quiet water seems to hush itself to listen. Never so tender a cry is uttered by any bird I know ; it is the most exquisitely beautiful, caressing tone, heard in the dewy silence of morning and evening. He has many and varied notes and calls, some collo-quial, some business-like, some meditative, and his cry of fear breaks my heart to hear when any evil threatens his beloved nest ; but this ten-der call, " Sweet, sweet," is the most enchanting sound, happy with a fullness of joy that never fails to bring a thrill to the heart that listens. It is like the voice of Love itself.

Then out of the high heaven above, at once one hears the happy chorus of the barn swallows ; they come rejoicing, their swift wings cleave the blue, they fill the air with woven melody of grace and music. Till late August they remain. Like the martins', their note is pure joy ; there is no coloring of sadness in any sound they make. The sandpiper's note is pensive with all its sweet-ness ; there is a quality of thoughtfulness, as it were, in the voice of the song-sparrow ; the robin has many sad cadences ; in the fairy bugling of the oriole there is a triumphant richness, but not

such pure delight; the blackbird's call is keen
and sweet, but not so glad; and the bobolink,
when he shakes those brilliant jewels of sound
from his bright throat, is always the prince of
jokers, full of fun, but not so happy as comical.
The swallows' twittering seems an expression of
unalloyed rapture, — I should select it from the
songs of all the birds I know as the voice of un-
shadowed gladness.

"OD Almightie first planted a Garden," says Lord Bacon. "And indeed it is the Purest of Humane Pleasures, it is the Greatest Refreshment to the Spirits of Man." Never were truer words spoken.

So deeply is the gardener's instinct implanted in my soul, I really love the tools with which I work, — the iron fork, the spade, the hoe, the rake, the trowel, and the watering-pot are pleasant objects in my eyes. The ingenuity of modern times has invented many variations of these primitive instruments of toil, and many of them are most useful and helpful, as, for instance, a short, five-pronged hand-fork, a delightful tool to use in breaking up the earth about the roots of weeds. Some of the weeds are so wide-spreading and tenacious, like clover and mallow, that they seem to have fastened themselves around the nether millstone, it is so difficult to disengage their hold. Once loosened, however, by the friendly little fork, they must come up, whether they will or no.

I like to take the hoe in my hands and break

to pieces the clods of earth left by the overturn-
ing spade, to work into the soil the dark, velvet-
smooth, scentless barn manure which is to furnish
the best of food for my flowers ; it is a pleasure
to handle the light rake, drawing it evenly through
the soil and combing out every stick and stone
and straw and lump, till the ground is as smooth
and fine as meal.   This done carefully and thoroughly, the beds laid out neatly, with their surface level as a floor, and not heaped high enough
to let the rains run off, — then is the ground
ready for the sowing of the seeds.

The very act of planting a seed in the earth
has in it to me something beautiful.   I always do
it with a joy that is largely mixed with awe.   I
watch my garden beds after they are sown, and
think how one of God's exquisite miracles is
going on beneath the dark earth out of sight.   I
never forget my planted seeds.   Often I wake in
the night and think how the rains and the dews
have reached to the dry shell and softened it; how
the spirit of life begins to stir within, and the individuality of the plant to assert itself ; how it is
thrusting two hands forth from the imprisoning
husk, one, the root, to grasp the earth, to hold
itself firm and absorb its food, the other stretching above to find the light, that it may drink in
the breeze and sunshine and so climb to its full
perfection of beauty.   It is curious that the leaf
should so love the light and the root so hate it.
In his " Proserpina " John Ruskin discourses on
this subject in his own inimitable way.   All he
says of this is most interesting and suggestive:

"The first instinct of the stem, . . . the instinct of seeking the light, as of the root to seek darkness — what words can speak the wonder of it?" If "the seed falls in the ground with the springing germ of it downwards, with heavenly cunning the taught stem curls round and seeks the never seen light." The "taught" stem! Who taught it? What he says of the leaves and stems is very beautiful; every one should read it. I really do not know which is most wonderful of these descriptions of his, but nothing could be more striking than this definition: "A root is a group of growing fibres which taste and suck what is good for the plant out of the ground, and by their united strength hold it in its place. . . . The thick limbs of roots do not feed, but only the fine ends of them, which are something between tongues and sponges, and while they absorb moisture readily, are yet as particular about getting what they think nice to eat as any dainty little boy or girl; looking for it everywhere, and turning angry and sulky if they don't get it."

There could not be a better description than this, and if any seedsman would like to make his fortune without delay, he has only to have printed on every packet of seed he offers for sale the kind of soil, the food, required by each plant. For instance, why not say of Mignonette, It flourishes best in a poor and sandy soil; so treated it is much more fragrant than in a rich earth, which causes it to run to leaves and makes its flowers fewer and less sweet. Or of Poppies, Plant them in a rich sandy loam, all except the Californias

(*Eschscholtzia*), which do best in a poor soil. Or of Pansies, Give them the richest earth you can find, no end of water, and partial shade. Or, Don't worry over drought for your Nasturtiums; they come from Chile and will live and thrive with less water than almost anything else that grows; don't trouble yourself to enrich the ground for them; that makes them profuse and coarse of leaves and sparing of flowers; leave them to shift for themselves, once having cleared them of weeds. No flower bears neglect so well. Or, Give your Zinnias a heavy soil; they like clay. Or, Keep Sweet Peas as wet as you can and make the ground for them as rich as possible. Or, Keep barn manure away from your Lilies for your life! they will not brook contact with it, but a rich soil they also like, only it must be made so by anything rather than stable manure, and they, too, like clay; they blossom best when it is given them. But transport to your garden a portion of the very barnyard itself in which to set Roses, Sunflowers and Hollyhocks, Honeysuckles and Dahlias. Hints of this kind would be to the unaccustomed tiller of the soil simply invaluable. How much they would lessen failures and discouragements! And to learn these things by one's self takes half a lifetime of sad experience.

To return to our planting. Yes, the sowing of a seed seems a very simple matter, but I always feel as if it were a sacred thing among the mysteries of God. Standing by that space of blank and motionless ground, I think of all it holds for me of beauty and delight, and I am filled with

joy at the thought that I may be the magician to
whom power is given to summon so sweet a pa-
geant from the silent and passive soil.   I bring a
mat from the house and kneel by the smooth bed
of mellow brown earth, lay a narrow strip of board
across it a few inches from one end, draw a furrow firmly and evenly in the ground along the
edge of the board, repeating this until the whole
bed is grooved at equal distances across its entire
length.   Into these straight furrows the living
seeds are dropped, the earth replaced over them
(with a depth of about twice their diameter), and
the board laid flat with gentle pressure over all
the surface till it is perfectly smooth again.   Then
must the whole be lightly and carefully watered.
With almost all the seeds sown in this bird-
blest and persecuted little garden, I am obliged
to lay newspapers or some protection over the
planted beds, and over these again sheets of wire
netting, to keep off the singing sparrows till the
seeds are safely sprouted.   Last year, one morning early in May, I put a border of Mignonette
seeds round every flower bed.   When I came to
the garden again in the afternoon, it was alive
with flirting wings and tails and saucy beaks and
bright eyes, and stout little legs and claws scratch-
ing like mad; all white-throats and song-sparrows, and hardly a seed had these merry little
marauders left in the ground.   Around the edge
of each bed a groove ran, nicely hollowed by their
industrious feet, and empty as my hopes.   I replaced the seed from my store, and this time took
great pains to lay two laths side by side over the

lines I had sowed, for safety. Next morning I found the birds again at it; they had burrowed under, kicked over, scratched away the light sticks, and again the seeds were all devoured. Patiently I planted once more, and this time dragged from a pile of lumber heavy square beams of different lengths, which I laid along the borders. The birds eyed the barricades, strove to burrow under, but were forced to give it up, and so at last I conquered. In the course of a week I turned over the protecting beams and found the little Mignonette plants white as potato shoots that have sprouted in a cellar, but safe, for which I was devoutly thankful! A day or two of sun and air made them green and strong, and all summer long I valued every fragrant spike of flowers they gave me, doubly, because of all the trouble I had gone through to save them. I mention this little episode merely to illustrate the fact that the would-be gardener requires more patience than most mortals!

The state of the weather, the temperature of the air, the amount of rain which falls, make all the difference in the world in the time it takes for the first green leaves to appear. Some seeds take longer than others to germinate: for instance, Hollyhocks, Marigolds, ten weeks Stocks or Gillyflowers, Rose of Heaven, Zinnias, and many others come up in from three to five days if all circumstances are favorable, that is, if it is warm, moist, and sunny enough; Asters, single Dahlias, Sunflowers, Cornflowers, Mignonette, Coreopsis, Morning-glory, Picotee Pinks, Wallflowers, Sweet

Williams, and by far the greater number of an-
nuals appear in from five to seven days; Balsams,
Pansies, Begonias, Drummond's Phlox, Poppies,
Verbenas, Thunbergia, and many others, in from
eight to ten days; Columbines, Flax, Artemisia,
Feverfew, Campanula, and so forth, in from ten to
twelve days; Maurandia, Forget-me-not, Petunia,
Lantana, Nicotiana (an exquisite flower, by the
way), in from twelve to fifteen days; Cobœa,
Gloxinia, Primroses, Geraniums, and others, in
from fifteen to twenty days; Perennial Phlox,
Clematis, Perennial Larkspurs (which are
heavenly!), and various others, take from twenty
to thirty-five days to germinate; and as for Lu-
pines and Lilies and Ampelopsis, and the like,
they take a whole year! But common gardeners
don't try to raise these from seed, fortunately.

With the first faint green lines that are visible
along the flower beds come the weeds, yea, and
even before them; a wild, vigorous, straggling
army, full of health, of strength, and a most marvelous power of growth. These must be dealt
with at once and without mercy; they must be
pulled up root and branch, without a moment's
delay. There is clover that appears with a little
circular leaf and has a root that seems to reach
all round in the under world; it goes everywhere
and holds on to the earth with a grip which is
unequaled by anything that grows. Not an atom
of its roots must be left in the ground, for every
thread of it will send up new shoots, and if not
watched fill all the space in a few weeks. Another
difficult weed to manage is the chickweed, which

is so delicate that it breaks at the slightest touch.
It is a most all-pervading weed; it fills every
space between the flowers, overruns them like a
green mist, and will surely strangle them if left
unmolested.   Alphonse Karr, who so greatly enjoyed his garden, and wrote of it with so much
pleasure, says: " The chickweed is endowed with
a fecundity that no other plant possesses. . . .
Seven or eight generations of chickweed cover
the earth every year. . . . It occupies the fields
naturally, and invades our gardens; it is almost
impossible to destroy it."

There is a long procession of weeds to be
fought: pigweed, ragweed, smartweed, shepherd's
purse, mallow, mustard, sorrel, and many more,
which make the first crop.   The second consists
largely of quitch-grass, the very worst of all, and
purslain or pusley, which Charles Dudley War-
ner has immortalized in his charming book, " My
Summer in a Garden."   The roots of quitch-
grass are as strong as steel and run rapidly in
all directions underneath the surface, sending
up tender shoots that break too easily when you
touch them.   The root must be found, grasped
firmly, and followed its whole length to utter extermination, or the grass will come up like a giant,
and later cannot be dealt with except by pulling
up also the flowers among which it inextricably
entangles itself.   The flat, olive-green leaves and
red fleshy stems of the pusley, running over the
ground in a mat, next appear; this is easily dis-
posed of, only it continues to come up, — fresh
plants in endless succession rise from the soil all

summer, and must be watched and faithfully destroyed.

There is one weed, or wild plant, dodder by
name, which has given my island garden the
greatest possible trouble. It is often wrongly
called gold-thread, because it looks like a tangled
mass of amber thread, but the true gold-thread is
quite different. The whole plant consists of nothing but these seemingly endless brittle reddish
yellow stalks with bunches of small, dull, whitish
flowers without stems, borne at intervals, with no
leaves at all. It has no root in the earth, it is a
parasite, and not at all particular as to what it
fastens itself upon; anything that comes in its
way will answer its purpose. It is very pretty in
its place, growing among the goldenrod and blue
skullcap at the top of the rocky little coves that
slope down to the water about the island, throwing itself from plant to plant, and making a mass
of translucent amber color. But alas! when it
gets into a civilized garden, woe, woe unto that
garden! A handful of it in bloom was brought
to my piazza twenty years ago, and some of it
was accidentally thrown into the flower beds; I
have been fighting it ever since. I have never
yet been able to get rid of it! Next year I found
my Nasturtiums, Cornflowers, Marigolds, and all
the rest tangled together in this yellow web, a
mass of inextricable confusion. Year after year
I waged war against it, but even yet it is not entirely exterminated. I never allow a plant of it
in the garden, no seeds of it ripen there, and none
of it grows near the place outside; not a single

atom of it in my small domain could possibly escape my eye, and yet its seeds come up more or less every year; I am sure to find one or two plants of it in the garden somewhere. They emerge from the ground, each like a fine yellow hair, till they are an inch and a half or two inches long; they reach with might and main toward the nearest legitimate growing plant, and when they touch it cling to it like a limpet; then they draw their other end up out of the ground and set up housekeeping for the rest of their lives. They adhere to the unhappy individual upon which they have fixed themselves with a grip that grows more and more horrible; they suck all its juices, drink all its health and strength and beauty, and fling out trailers to the next and the next and the next, till the whole garden is a mass of ruin and despair.

For many springs after the first year it appeared I used to take a glass tumbler and go all over the beds soon after they were laid out, pulling up these tiny yellow hairs, and in an hour or two I have pulled up five or six tumblers full. I gathered them in glasses so that I might be quite sure of all I plucked, and because they could not easily blow away out of such a receptacle. For wherever they might fall, if they touched a green growing thing they would in an astonishingly short space of time make themselves fast for good, or rather for ill! Every year I watch for it with the most eager vigilance as I weed carefully over the whole surface of the little pleasance, but sometimes it steals up after all the weeding

is done, and, before I know it, I find it has begun
to tie the flowers together. Then I pull up all
the plants it has touched, lay them in a basket,
carry them down, and cast the whole into the sea.
It is the only way to be rid of it. I have known
it wind its inexorable way tightly up the large
smooth stem of a tall Sunflower, where I had not
thought of looking for it, till there was not an
atom of the skin of the stalk visible, only amber-
colored dodder and its white, dull flowers from
the great head of the blossoming Sunflower tree
to its root. Into the sea the whole thing went, at
once, without a moment of delay!

These are only a few of the weeds with which
one must battle, though dodder, I fancy, seldom
troubles any one on the planet as it does me. It
takes an island garden to produce so remarkable
a growth! Most of them soon become familiar,
too familiar, indeed, and at last one learns how to
manage them. The great mistake which the
inexperienced gardener makes is in leaving a
morsel of the root of a weed in the ground. Only
by combing the earth through and through between the rows of plants with the small hand-fork
(after all the intruders have been removed as
carefully as possible with the hand), can you be
sure that they are gone. Other seeds of weeds
will be overturned and brought to the surface in
the process, and these will sprout in their turn,
but by this time the flowers will have made so
much headway that they will crowd out the new
crop of weeds enough to insure their own safety,
except in some few instances. Apple of Peru

(Stramonium) is one of the most powerful and
persistent among the enemies; a poisonous thing
with a loathsome odor, it must be watched for
and routed, which fortunately is easily done.   In
its perfected growth this is the most uncanny
plant, — a strong, low bush with bat-like leaves
of dark green, and long, pale lavender, lily-like
flowers, followed by a round spiked seed-vessel.
Says Hawthorne: "What hidden virtue is in
these things that it is granted to sow themselves
with the wind and to grapple the earth with this
immitigable stubbornness, and to flourish in spite
of obstacles, and never to suffer blight beneath
any sun or shade, but always to mock their enemies with the same wicked luxuriance?"   Mrs.
Gatty (the mother of that beautiful woman,
Juliana Horatia Ewing, who has so discoursed on
the subject of flowers and many other things as
to make all time her debtor) answers the question, "What is a weed?" by this statement, "A
weed is a plant out of place."   A keen and close
observer of nature says: "A better definition
would be, 'A plant which has an innate disposi-
tion to *get* into the wrong place;'" and goes on
to say: "This is the very essence of weed character — in plants as in men.   If you glance through
your botanical books you will see often added to
certain names, 'a troublesome weed.'   It is not
its being venomous or ugly, but its being imper-
tinent — thrusting itself where it has no business
and hinders other people's business — that makes
a weed of it. . . .   Who ever saw a wood anemone
or a heath blossom out of place? . . .   What is it,

then, this temper in some plants — malicious as
it seems, intrusive, at all events, or erring —
which brings them out of their places, thrusts
them where they thwart us and offend?" This
seems to me the best definition of what constitutes a weed that I have seen.

And their strength is mighty, and their name
is legion. If there were no other enemies which
the gardener must fight, this one of weeds alone
is quite enough to tax all his powers and patience.

Then the plants kill each other if they are left
to grow as thickly together as the seeds were
sown; they must be "thinned out" as soon as
they have attained to their second leaf, leaving
two, three, four, or five inches between each two
plants side by side. I always leave two plants
where one would be enough, because something
is so likely to happen to destroy them, and if
there are two the hard fates may perhaps leave
one. Some things require much more space
than others. Pinks that spire up so thin and tall
can be set closer together than Poppies, which
spread widely in all directions. This pulling up
and throwing away of the superfluous plants is a
very difficult thing for me to do. I cannot bear
to destroy one of the precious young seedlings
that I have watched and tended with such love
and care, but it must be done. It is a matter of
the very greatest importance. The welfare of the
garden depends on it. I comfort myself as best
I may by saving all that will bear transplanting,
and then giving them away to the flower plots of
my fellow-gardeners on neighboring islands.

Soon the whole plot mantles over all its surface with the rich, warm green of vigorous leaf-
age. The new growth rejoices. That is the
right word for it. The gladness of green growing
things is apparent to any seeing eye. They rejoice with a radiant joy in sun and rain and air
and dew, in all care and kindness. They know
and respond to everything that is done for them.
The low-growing Drummond's Phlox is one of
the most satisfactory flowers for a beginner in the
art of gardening. There is no such word as fail
in its bright lexicon; and it blossoms continually
from the last of June till frost. Looking carefully every day, by the last half of June I find the
pale clustered flower buds showing; then it is
not long to wait before the whole bed is a blaze
of varied color, a delicate woven carpet of myriad
vivid hues. In the lovely buds the petals are
folded one over the other in beautiful succession.
The flowers are five-petaled, with a faint, sweet
perfume; they are borne in flat clusters of an
exquisite, velvety texture, with a clearly marked
eye in the centre encircling the few pearl-white
stamens; this eye varies with the hue of each
different flower. There will be delicious pinks
among these Phloxes, from the palest rose to the
deepest cherry; all shades of red from bright,
light scarlet, clear and pure, to a rich black red, —
the Black Warrior. There will be all heavenly
purples, pale lilacs, deep red purple and blue
purple, perfect snow white: the eye in this last is
soft green, like the touches on a Snowdrop bell.
The scarlet flowers have a ring of black-red about

the centre, delicately gorgeous. There are almost
endless varieties and mixtures of color; they are
full of surprises. The Star of Quedlinburg is
such a pretty, quaint change rung upon this
pleasant theme of Phloxes. The centre of the
outer line of each petal is drawn out at the edge
like the tails on the under wings of the Luna
moth. These long tails in which each petal ter-
minates give the flower the aspect of a star with
rays. "Ask of Nature why the star form she
repeats," says Emerson. It is forever repeated
among the flowers.

At bird-peep, as the country folk have a charming way of calling the break of day, I am in my
dear garden, — planting and transplanting, hoeing,
raking, weeding, watering, tying up and training
those plants that need it, and always fighting for
their precious lives against their legions of enemies. There is a time of great danger upon the
island from the birds when they are migrating
northward. They come suddenly down from the
sky in myriads, on their way to the continent,
and I have known them to strip the little plot of
every green shoot in a single day, utterly bare.
Nothing but fishing nets draped over the whole
space will save the garden when these hungry
hordes descend. But I do not lose patience with
the birds, however sorely they try me. I love
them too well. How should they know that the
garden was not planted for them? Those be-
longing to the thrush tribe are the most mis-
chievous; the others do not disturb the flower
beds so much. The friendly robin, though a

thrush, only comes for worms, to which he is more than welcome. Most of the other birds — bobolinks, kingbirds, orioles, purple finches, and many other beautiful creatures less familiar — stay with us for a short time only, on their passage north or south every year; but a single pair of kingbirds build every summer in the one tall elm-tree on the island, where also builds a cosy nuthatch and raises a numerous family, and one pair of most interesting kingfishers haunts the upper cove till late in the season. A Maryland yellow-throat began building here last summer. For several years one pair of cuckoos lingered through the summer, but at last ceased to come. A few blackbirds build, the white-throats stay late, but several varieties of swallows, the song-sparrows, and sandpipers remain and rear their broods. How we wish the robins would stay too, and the orioles and all the sweet company! But there are no trees to shelter them. Their coming and going, however, is a matter of the greatest interest to the little family on the island, and we are thrown into a state of the deepest excitement by the apparition of a scarlet tanager, or a rose-breasted grosbeak, or any of those unfamiliar beauties. Once a ferruginous thrush came and stayed a week with us in early June. Every day when he perched on a ridge-pole or chimney-top and sang, the whole family turned out in a body to listen, making a business of it, attending to nothing else while that thrilling melody was poured out on the silent air. That was a gift of the gods which we could, none of us, afford to neglect!

Says the wise Lord Bacon again: "And because the Breath of Flowers is far sweeter in the
Aire (when it comes and goes, like the Warbling
of Music) than in the hand, therefore nothing is
more fit for that delight than to know what be
the Flowers and Plants that doe best perfume the
Aire."

The most exquisite perfume known to my garden is that of the Wallflowers; there is nothing
equal to it. They blossom early, and generally
before June has passed they are gone, and have
left me mourning their too swift departure. I
wonder they are not more generally cultivated,
but I fancy the fact that they do not blossom till
the second year has much to do with their rarity.
It requires so much more faith and patience to
wait a whole year, and meanwhile carefully watch
and tend the plants, excepting during the time
when winter covers them with a blanket of snow;
but when at last spring comes and the tardy
flowers appear, then one is a thousand times re-
paid for all the tedious months of waiting. They
return such wealth of bloom and fragrance for
the care and thought bestowed on them! Their
thick spikes of velvet blossoms are in all shades
of rich red, from scarlet to the darkest brown,
from light gold to orange; some are purple; and
their odor, — who shall describe it! Violets,
Roses, Lilies, Sweet Peas, Mignonette, and Helio-
trope, with a dash of Honeysuckle, all mingled
in a heavenly whole. There is no perfume which
I know that can equal it. And they are so lavish
of their scent; it is borne off the garden and

wafted everywhere, into the house and here and
there in all directions, in viewless clouds on the
gentle air. To make a perfect success of Wallflowers they must be given lime in some form
about the roots. They thrive marvelously if fed
with a mixture of old plastering in the soil, or
bone meal, or, if that is not at hand, the meat
bones from the kitchen, calcined in the oven and
pounded into bits, stirred in around the roots is
fine for them. This treatment makes all the difference in the world in their strength and beauty.
After the Wallflowers, Roses and Lilies, Mignonette, Pinks, Gillyflowers, Sweet Peas, and the
Honeysuckles for fragrance, and of these last, the
monthly Honeysuckle is the most divine. Such
vigor of growth I have never seen in any other
plant, and it is hardy even without the least protection in our northern climate. It climbs the
trellis on my piazza and spreads its superb clusters of flowers from time to time all summer.
Each cluster is a triumph of beauty, flat in the
centre and curving out to the blossoming edge in
joyous lines of loveliness, most like a wreath of
heavenly trumpets breathing melodies of perfume
to the air. Each trumpet of lustrous white
deepens to a yellower tint in the centre where the
small ends meet; each blossom where it opens at
the lip is tipped with fresh pink; each sends out
a group of long stamens from its slender throat
like rays of light; and the whole circle of radiant
flowers has an effect of gladness and glory indescribable: the very sight of it lifts and refreshes
the human heart. And for its odor, it is like the

spirit of romance, sweet as youth's tender dreams.
It is summer's very soul.

This beautiful vine will grow anywhere, for anybody, only give it half a chance, such is its matchless vigor. I wonder why it is not found in every
garden; nothing so well repays the slightest care.

Next in power come the Sweet Peas, blossoming
the livelong summer in all lovely tints save only
yellow, and even that the kind called Primrose
approaches, with its faint gold suffusion of both
inner and outer petals. I plant them by myriads
in my tiny garden — all it will hold. Transplant,
I should say, because of my friends the birds, who
never leave me one if I dare plant them out of
doors. But this transplanting is most delightful.
I thoroughly enjoy digging with the hoe a long
trench six inches deep for the strong young seedlings, lifting them from the boxes, carefully disen-
tangling their long white roots each from the other
as I take them out, and placing them in a close
row the whole length of the deep furrow, letting
the roots drop their whole length, with no curling
or crowding, then half filling the hollow with
water, drawing the earth about the roots and
firming the whole with strong and gentle touch.
They do not droop a single leaf so transplanted;
they go on growing as if nothing had happened,
if only they are given all the water they need.
Already they stretch out their delicate tendrils to
climb, and I love to give them for support the
sticks with which the farmers supply their pea
vines for the market; but on my island are no
woods, so I am thankful for humble bayberry and

elder branches for the purpose. It is another
pleasure to go afar among the rocks for these and
wheel them to the flower beds in a light wheelbarrow, which is one of the most useful things
one can possess for work about the garden. At
once the vines lay hold of the slender sticks and
climb to the very top, fain are they to go much
farther. But I cut the tops so that they may
branch from the sides and keep within bounds,
and they soon make a solid hedge of healthy
green. Oh, when the blossoms break from these
green hedges like heavenly winged angels, and
their pure, cool perfume fills the air, what joy is
mine!

I find Sweet Peas can hardly have too rich a
soil, provided always that they are kept sufficiently
wet. They *must* have moisture, their roots must
be kept cool and damp, — a mulch of leaves or
straw is a very good thing to keep the roots from
drying, — and they must always be planted as deep
as possible. Wood ashes give them a stronger
growth. Their colors, the great variety of them,
and their vivid delicacy are wonderful; they are
most beautiful against the background of the sea;
they are a continual source of delight, and never
cease to bloom, with me, if gathered every day and
watered abundantly, the whole summer long, even
through the autumn till November. But they
must never be suffered to go to seed; that would
check their blossoming at once. I revel in their
beauty week after week, bringing them into the
house and arranging them in masses every other
day. Clear glass vases are most effective for

them, and they look loveliest, I think, when each
color is kept by itself. For the Princess Beatrice,
which is a divine pale pink, a shade of rose re-
fined and exquisite, there are glasses of clear pink
that repeat the hues of the flowers with magical
gradations and reflections. For the white kinds
there are white vases, the most effective of ground
glass, the opaque surface of which matches the
tone of the flowers.

Of the named kinds of Sweet Peas the most
beautiful shades of pink that I know are the
divinely delicate Princess Beatrice, the palest
rose-color; Adonis, a deeper pink, very clear
and rich; the Orange Prince, a most ineffably
splendid color of bright yellow-rose; these together
make a combination of color that satisfies the inmost soul. Carmine Invincible is the most
splendid red; the Butterfly is white edged with
mauve, and combined with the delicate rose
Princess Beatrice makes a delicious harmony.
Blanche Ferry is also a lovely rose. Queen Vic-
toria is the best white I have known; but every
year new varieties are found which seem more and
more beautiful, and it is only by trying them that
one finds which to depend on.

Of the worth of these I have mentioned I am
sure; they are the strongest growers, the freest
bloomers, and the most beautiful of their kind.
They never disappoint you if you give them the
right care. The list of flowers in my island garden is by no means long, but I could discourse of
them forever! They are mostly the old-fashioned
flowers our grandmothers loved. Beginning with

Snowdrops, Crocuses, Daffodils, Narcissus, a few Hyacinths, Scillas, an English Primrose or two, Tulips, and several other early blooming plants, one big red Peony, Columbine, Ragged Robin, Cornflowers, Roses and Lilies, Larkspurs, Pinks and Gillyflowers, Sweet Williams, Wallflowers, Forget-me-nots, single Dahlias, Sunflowers of every kind, and Hollyhocks of all colors, Poppies in almost endless variety, Nasturtiums of all hues, pot Marigolds, summer Chrysanthemums in great variety, Rose Campion, or Rose of Heaven, Pansies, Phlox, Sweet Peas, and Mignonette, Crimson Flax and the tall blue Perennial Flax (a wonderful blue!), many kinds of Coreopsis, — all most valuable and decorative, — Asters, Honeysuckle and Clematis, Morning-glories, Lavender and Foxgloves, Candytuft, Verbenas, Thunbergia, Pentstemon, the heaven-blue Ipomea, white Petunias, — because they are so beautiful by moonlight, — a few Four-o'clocks, and so forth. These are enough for a most happy little garden. A few more modern plants are added, a golden and a rosy Lily from Japan, a lustrous white gold-hearted Anemone from the same country, for autumn blooming, one or two tuberous-rooted Begonias, some Gaillardias and Zinnias, the fragrant little Asperula (Woodruff), and some others. Among the new plants one of the most interesting is the Hugelia Cœrulea, which grows a foot and a half high, with a many-branched woolly leaf, and flowers in flat clusters of the most delicious light blue. This is a flower with an atmosphere; it has a quality of beauty quite indescribable.

I COPY the notes of a few days' work in the garden in May, just to give an idea of their character and of the variety of occupation in this small space of ground.

May 11. This morning at four o'clock the sky was one rich red blush in the east, over a sea as calm as a mirror. How could I wait for the sun to lift its scarlet rim above the dim sea-line (though it rose punctually at forty-seven minutes past four), when my precious flower beds were waiting for me! It was not possible, and I was up and dressed before he had flooded the earth with glory. "Straight was a path of gold for him," I said, as I gazed out at the long line of liquid splendor along the ocean. All the boxes and baskets of the more delicate seedlings were to be put out from my chamber window on flat house-top and balcony, they and the forest of Sweet Peas to be thoroughly watered, and the Pansies half shaded with paper lest the sun should work them woe. At five the household was stirring, there was time to write a letter or two, then came breakfast before six, and by half past six I was out of doors at work in the vast

46

circle of motionless silence, for the sea was too calm for me to hear even its breathing. It was so beautiful, — the dewy quiet, the freshness, the long, still shadows, the matchless, delicate, sweet charm of the newly wakened world. Such a color as the grass had taken on during the last few warm days; and where the early shadows lay long across it, such indescribable richness of tone! There was so much for me to do, I hardly knew where to begin. At the east of the house the bed of Pansies set out yesterday was bright with promise, every little plant holding itself gladly erect. I began with the trellis each side of the steps leading down into the garden, and first set out a Coboea Scandens, one to the right and one to the left, — strong, sturdy plants which I had been keeping weeks in the house till it should be warm enough to trust them out of doors. They were a foot high and stretching their sensitive tendrils in all directions, seeking something for support. They grasped the trellis at once and seemed to spread out every leaf to the warm sun, while I poured cool water and liquid manure about their roots, and congratulated them on their escape into the open ground. Near them, against the same trellis, I put down two Tropæolum Lobbianum Lucifers, a new scarlet variety of these delicate Nasturtiums, that they might climb together over the broad arch. Some time ago I had planted there also some Mexican Morning-glories sent me by an unknown friend, and if they come up, and Coboea, Nasturtiums, and Morning-glories all climb together and clasp hands with Honeysuckle, Wistaria, and Wild Cucumber, my porch will, indeed, be a bower of beauty! Then against wall and fence I set out the stout bushes of single Dahlias which have been growing ever since last January. A new variety called Star of Lyons interests me. I am anxious to know what it is like, what its color, what its shape. It is such a pleasure always to be finding new varieties and combinations, fresh surprises in unfamiliar flowers. Seeking the smallest posy bed I own, into this I transplanted another stranger, Papaver Alpinum Roseum, a rose-colored Iceland Poppy. How I shall watch it grow, and how eagerly wait for it to blossom! Eight egg-shells full of it were set down and carefully watered. Next, a row of baby Wallflowers were established in a long line near the tall ones that are thick with buds. I am going to try to have a succession of bloom from these, if it can be accomplished, all summer. In another bed I began to set out a few of the choicest Sweet Peas, the new kinds; these were already a foot long from tip to root ends. I have no words to tell what pleasant work this is! After the Sweet Peas were comfortably settled, I covered the whole bed with a length of light mosquito net, pegging it at the corners, laying sticks and stones along the edges to hold it down, so that the saucy sparrows should find no loophole by which to wriggle inside, they having watched the whole process with interested eyes from their perch on the fence-rail. How beautiful it was to be sitting there in the sweet weather, working in the wholesome brown earth! Just be-

yond the Sweet Peas I could see my strong white
Lilies springing up, a foot high already, with the
splendid hardy Larkspurs behind them, prom-
ising a wealth of white and gold and azure by
and by. From time to time through the calm
morning, as I labored thus peacefully, I heard the
loons laughing loud and clear in the stillness,
and by lifting my head could see them off the
end of the wharf at the landing swimming to and
fro with their bright reflections, catching no end
of fish and having the most delightful time, —
every now and then half raising themselves from
the water and flapping their wings, showing the
dazzling white with which the strong pinions
were lined, and laughing again and again with a
wild and eerie sound. This means that a storm
is coming, I know. But I love to hear them, and
how devoutly thankful I am that there is not a
creature with a gun on this blessed island! The
loons know it well, or they never would venture
in so near, while they shout to the morning their
wild cries.

Near me, where I had made the earth so very
wet, suddenly fluttered down a ruddy-breasted
barn swallow, the beauty! for on such heavenly
terms are we that he did not mind me in the
least as he gathered a tiny load of mud for his
nest against the rafters in the barn, and flew away
with it low on the wind. The barn swallows do
not visit my small inclosure as often as do my
nearer neighbors, the white-breasted martins.

All this time the lovely day was slowly changing its early delicate colors and freshness for the

whiter light of noon.   By twelve o'clock the wind
had "hauled" from west to south, going round
through the east, and sending millions of light
ripples across the glassy water, deepening its
color to sparkling sapphire, and at last the sun
overhead seemed to pelt quicksilver in floods
upon it, and then it was dinner-time.   After an
hour of rest again I took up my work.   All
about, here and there and everywhere, I dug up
the scattered Echinocystus vines and set them
against the house, so that they could run up the
trellises on all sides to make grateful shade by
and by.   A few straying Primroses waited to be
moved outside the fence, — they take up so much
room within, and room is so precious inside the
garden.   Young plants of the charming, old-fashioned Sweet Rocket had to be collected from the
nooks where they had sown themselves far and
near, and set in clumps in corners.   Then there
was a box of white Forget-me-nots some one had
sent me, to be established in their places, and I
finished the afternoon by planting Shirley Poppies all up and down the large bank at the southwest of the garden, outside.   I am always planting
Shirley Poppies somewhere!   One never can
have enough of them, and by putting them into
the ground at intervals of a week, later and later,
one can secure a succession of bloom and keep
them for a much longer time, — keep, indeed, their
heavenly beauty to enjoy the livelong summer, —
whereas, if they are all planted at once you would
see them for a blissful moment, a week or ten
days at most, and then they are gone.   I have

planted and am going to continue planting till the middle of June, in this year of grace 1893, no less than two whole ounces of Shirley Poppies in all, and when one reflects that the seeds are so small as to be hardly more than visible to the naked eye, one realizes this to be a great many.

May 12th. Again a radiant day. I watched the thin white half ring of the waning moon as it stole up the east through the May haze at dawn. This kind of haze belongs especially to this month; it is such an exquisite color, like ashes of roses, till the sun suffuses it with a burning blush before he leaps alive from the ocean's rim. Again in the garden at a little after six, to find the sparrows busy tunneling up and down the bank, devouring the Poppies that I planted yesterday. How they can see the seeds at all, or why they should care to feast on anything so small, or why they do not all perish, as poor Pillicoddy proposed doing, from the effects of such doses of opium, passes my understanding. There was nothing to be done but to plant them all over and then trail through the dewy grass long boards to lay up and down, covering the bank, for protection.

First, there were the small Tea Rosebushes to be set out in their sunny bed, made rich with finely sifted manure and soot and a sprinkling of wood ashes. And here let me say that all through the spring, beginning when the hardy Damask and Jacqueminots, etc., are just unfolding their leaf buds, it is a most excellent plan to sift wood ashes quite thickly over all the Rose-

bushes, either just after a shower or after you
have been sprinkling them; let it remain on
them for several hours, — if the sun is not shining
I leave it half a day, — but then it must all be
carefully washed off, every trace of it, or it will
spoil the leaves.   This kills or discourages all
sorts of insect pests, and the effect of the ashes
on the soil about their roots is most beneficial to
the Roses.

As I sat in measureless content by the little
flower bed, carefully slipping my pretty Bon
Silenes and Catherine Mermets and yellow Sun-
sets and the rest out of their pots, and gently
firming them in the ground, with plenty of water
for refreshment, a cloud of the most delicious
perfume brooded about me from a bed of white
violets at the left, the hardiest, faithfulest, friend-
liest little flowers in the world.   I found two
small Polyantha Roses had lived all winter in this
sheltered bed; that was indeed a charming find!
At the back of it grows a tall Jacqueminot, a
black Tuscany Rose, and the strong white Rosa
Rugosa, a Japanese variety which bears very
large single flowers in the greatest profusion.
This Rose is extremely valuable, easily obtained,
so hardy as to be almost indestructible, and absolutely untroubled by any disease or insect plague
whatever.   Its foliage is always fresh and handsome, and its seed vessels are huge scarlet balls
as large as an average Crab-Apple, most ornamental after the flowers are gone.   But the old, old
black Tuscany Rose is the most precious of all.
Mine came from an ancient garden that vanished

long ago, but which used to be a glory to the town in which it grew. It is a hardy Rose also, in color so darkly red as to be almost black, — a warm red, less crimson than scarlet, glowing with a kind of smouldering splendor, with only two rows of petals round a centre of richest gold. At the end of this bed is a Water Hyacinth floating in its tub, and near it, in another tub, a large pink Water Lily, kept over from last summer in a frost-proof cellar, is sending up the loveliest leaves, touched with so sweet a crimson as to be almost as delightful as the blossoms themselves. All the rest of this day was spent in transplanting Asters from boxes into the beds all over the garden, edging nearly every bed with them, so that when the fleeting glory of Poppies and other earlier annuals is gone there will still be beautiful color to gladden our eyes late in the summer, quite into the autumn days.

In the afternoon I had all the many boxes of Sweet Peas brought to the piazza to be ready for transplanting, but remembering the sparrows, I covered each box carefully with mosquito netting before leaving them for the night.

14th. Sunday. A storm of wild wind and flooding rain, the storm the loons predicted! At breakfast my gardening brother said, " Well, my sweet peas are all gone!" "Oh," I cried in the greatest sympathy, "what has happened to them?" for he had planted six pounds or more, and they had come up finely. "Sparrows," was his laconic reply. I flew to my boxes on the piazza: they were safe, only through a tiny crack

in the net over one a bird had wriggled its little
body, and pulled up and flung the plants to right
and left all over the steps.   But my brother's long
rows, so green last night, were bare except for
broken stems and withering leaves.   Alas, it is so
much trouble to cover such a large area with netting, he thought this time he would trust to luck,
or Providence, or whatever one chooses to call it,
but it is a fatal thing to do.   Now he has to
plant all over again, even though I shall share my
boxes with him, and it will make his garden very
late indeed.   This time he will not fail to put
nets over all!   I sat on the piazza sheltered from
the rain and watched the birds.   Unmindful of
the tempest, they skipped gayly round the garden,
over and round the steps, examined all the tucked
up boxes of Sweet Peas, wished they could get in,
but finding it out of the question gave it up and
resigned themselves to the inevitable.   To and
fro, here and there they went, peering into every
nook and corner, behind every leaf and stick and
board and stalk, busily pecking away and devouring something with the greatest industry.   I
drew nearer to discover what it could be, and to
my great joy found it was the slugs which the
rain had called forth from their hiding-places;
the birds were working the most comprehensive
slaughter among them.   At that pleasing sight
I forgave them on the spot all their trespasses
against me.

15th.   A thick fog wrapped the world in dim-
ness early this morning; at eight o'clock it was
rolling off and piling itself in glorious headlands

over the coast, gleaming snow white in the sun,
but here and there thin silver strips lay across
distant sails and islands, lingering as if loath to
leave the earth for the sky. I took the baskets
of plants I had found necessary to dig up to give
the rest room, and paddled across to the next
island in a little lapstreaked dory, to give them
to my neighbors for their flower plots. Great is
the pleasure in the giving and the taking. It was
such a heavenly morning, so blue and calm after
the tumult of yesterday! Along the far-off coast
the joyous hills seemed laughing in the sunshine,
and the great sea rippled all over with smiles.

From the low shores of the islands came the
singing of the birds over the still water, with an
indescribably quiet and peaceful effect, and as I
rowed into the cove of my destination, passing
the coasts of the little island called Malaga, I saw
outlined against the sky the lovely grasses already blossoming among the rocks. A kingbird
sat on a bowlder and meditated; there was no tree,
so he was fain to be content with a rock to sit on.
I passed him almost near enough to touch him
with my oar, but he did not stir, not he! My
errand done and the plants distributed, I hastened
back to my own dear little plot again, and up and
down all the paths I went, digging out every
unwelcome root of grass, plantain, mallow, cat-
nip, clover, and the rest, once more raking them
clear and clean. Outside, in a bed by itself, I
sunk four pots of repotted Chrysanthemums, to
be ready for the windows in early winter. All
along the piazza are the house plants waiting to

be attended to, cut back, repotted, and the soil enriched for winter blooming. Every day I attend to them, a few at a time. I cannot spare much time from my planting, weeding, watering, transplanting, and so forth, in the garden, but soon they will be all done. Began to transplant a few of the hundreds of the main body of Sweet Pea plants into the ground, carefully covering each bed as I finished with breadths of light mosquito netting to make them sparrow-proof. As I was working busily I heard the sweet calling of curlews, and looking up saw six of them wheeling overhead. Such sociable birds! They replied to my challenge as if I had been one of themselves, and as long as their calls were answered, lingered near, but being forgotten presently drifted off on the wind, their clear whistle sounding fainter and fainter as they were lost in the distance. All the rest of this day was spent in setting out Sweet Peas, and it will take more than a whole day more to finish, for I put them all round against the fence outside, and into every space I can spare for them within. After tea I hunted slugs as usual, and scattered ashes and lime, but I really feel that my friends the toads have done me the inestimable favor of reducing their hideous numbers, for certainly there are less than last year so far. Early in April, as I was vigorously hoeing in a corner, I unearthed a huge toad, to my perfect delight and satisfaction; he had lived all winter, he had doubtless fed on slugs all the autumn. I could have kissed him on the spot! Very carefully I placed him in the middle of a large green clump of tender Columbine. He really was n't more than half awake, after his long winter nap, but he was alive and well, and when later I went to look after him, lo! he had crept off, perhaps to snuggle into the earth once more for another nap, till the sun should have a little more power.

To our great joy the frogs that we imported last year are also alive. We heard the soft rippling of their voices with the utmost pleasure; it is a lovely liquid-sweet sound. They have not lived over a winter here before. We feared that the vicinity of so much salt water might be injurious to them, but this year they have survived, and perhaps they may be established for good.

May 20th. All the past days have been filled with transplanting and the most vigorous weeding. In these five days the Sweet Peas have grown so tall I was obliged to go after sticks for them to-day, wheeling my light wheelbarrow up over the hill and across the island toward the south, where among the old ruined walls of cellars and houses, and little, almost erased garden plots, the thick growth of Bayberry and Elder offered me all the sticks I needed. Such a charming business was this! So beautiful the narrow road all the way, bordered by the lovely Shadbush in bridal white, the delicate red Cherry with flowers so like Hawthorn as to be frequently mistaken for it, the pink Chokecherry, the common Wild Cherry (which seems to attract to itself most of the caterpillars in the land), all blossoming for dear life, and among thickets of Blackberry, Raspberry, Gooseberry, Wild Currant, Winterberry, Spirea, and I know not what, such crowds of flowers! The last of the gay golden Erythroniums, the Dogtooth Violets, dancing in the breeze; the large, softly colored Anemones, now nearing their end; the banks of pearly Eyebrights; the white Violets, lowly and fragrant; the straw-colored Uvularia; the ivory spikes of Solomon's Seal, just breaking into bloom, with its companion, the starry Trientalis; the tufts of Fern in cool clefts of rocks, — of these I gathered several clumps for my fernery in the shade of the piazza. It would take too long to tell of all the flowers I saw, but one more I must mention. At the upper edge of a little cove at the southwest, where the old settlement of more than a hundred years ago was thickest, the earth was blue with the pretty Gill-go-over-the-ground, its charming blossoms covering the green turf and cropping out among the loose stones, — a dear, quaint little flower in two shades of blue marked with rich red-purple. It was too early for the Pimpernel to be in bloom, but the pink Herb Robert was out, the smallest of all the Geranium family, and I saw ranks of Goldenrod more than a foot high getting ready for autumn. To tell all I saw and all I loved and rejoiced in would take a whole day. Oh, the green and brown and golden mosses, the lovely, lowly growths along the way, and oh, the birds that sang and the waves that leaped and murmured along the shore! The sweet sky and the soft clouds, the far sails, the full joy of the summer morning, who shall tell it? I was so happy trundling home my barrow load of sticks piled to toppling, and finally tipping it up at the garden gate! It took the whole afternoon to stick the Peas, and I enjoyed every moment of it. Before putting the dry brittle branches in the ground, with a small, light hoe I went all over and through the earth about the Sweet Peas, uprooting chickweed and clover, pigweed and dogfennel, till there was not a weed to be seen near them. When night fell I had only just finished this pleasant work.

21st. Weeding all day in the hot sun; hard work, but pleasant. I find it the best way to lay two boards down near the plot I have to weed, and on them spread a waterproof, or piece of carpet, and kneeling or half reclining on this, get my face as close to my work as possible. Sitting flat on these boards, I weed all within my reach, then roll up a bit of carpet not bigger than a flat-iron holder, put it at the edge of the space I have cleared, and lean my elbow on it; that gives me another arm's-length that I can reach over, and so I go on till all is done. I move the rest for my elbow here and there as needed among the flowers. It takes me longer to weed than most people, because I will do it so thoroughly. It is such a pleasure and satisfaction to clear the beautiful brown earth, smooth and soft, from these rough growths, leaving the beautiful green Poppies and Larkspurs and Pinks and Asters, and the rest, in undisturbed possession! Now come the potent heats that preface summer, and everything grows and expands so fast, the process of thinning the crowded plants must begin forthwith. Oh, for days twice as long! Yet these approach the longest days of the year.

22d. Another glorious day of heat; the sun fairly drove me into the shade to work among the house plants on the piazza. Hot, hot, and bright, and outside the garden growing things begin to pine for showers. When the sun declined toward the west in the afternoon, I sat in the shade and from the veranda turned the hose with its fine sprinkler all over the garden. Oh, the joy of it! The delicious scents from earth and leaves, the glitter of drops on the young green, the gratitude of all the plants at the refreshing bath and draught of water! The rich red Wallflowers sent up fresh clouds of incense, the brilliant and delicate Iceland Poppies bowed their lovely heads and swayed with pleasure at the bright shower. But rain is greatly needed, searching rain which shall drench the ground and reach the roots, and give new life to everything.

23d. Again hot, still, and splendid. Spent all the morning hammering stakes down into the beds near Hollyhocks, Sunflowers, Larkspurs, Lilies, Roses, single Dahlias, and all the tall growing things. Many were tall enough to fasten to the stakes, — all will be, presently. One enormous red Hollyhock grew thirteen feet high by actual measurement before it stopped last year, in a corner near the piazza. Oh, but he was superb! At night the lights from one window streamed through a leafy arch of clambering vine, and illumined him as he swayed to and fro in the wind, a stately column of beauty and grace. A black-red

comrade leaned against him and mingled its rich blossoms with his brighter color, and near him were rose, pink, and cherry, and white spikes of bloom, lovely to behold.

All the afternoon weeding and thinning out the plants. The large bank sloping to the southwest outside the garden is a perfect mass of flowers to be, — no weeds, for I have conquered them; but it is next to impossible to pull up plants enough to give all room. Again and again I have thinned them; now I think I must leave them to their fate and let it be a case of survival of the fittest.

24th. Last night, after having given myself the pleasure of watering the garden, I could not sleep for anxiety about the slugs. I seldom water the flowers at night because the moisture calls them out, and they have an orgy feasting on my most precious children all night long. Before going to bed I went all over the inclosure and, alas, I found them swarming on the Sweet Peas; baby slugs, tiny creatures covering the tender leaves and the dry pea-sticks even, thick as grains of sand. I was in despair, and though I knew they did not mind ashes, I took the fine sifter and covered Peas, sticks, slugs, and all with a thick, smothering cloud of wood ashes. Then I left them with many misgivings and went to bed, but not to sleep, for thinking of them. At twelve o'clock I said to myself, You know the slugs don't care a rap for all the ashes in the world, but the friendly toads may be kept away by them, and who knows if such a smother of them may not kill the precious Peas themselves? I could not bear it any longer, rose up and donned my dress-ing gown, and out into the dark and dew I bore the hose, over my shoulders coiled, to the very farthest corners of the garden, and washed off every atom of ashes in the black midnight, and came back and slept in peace.

These are most anxious times on account of the slugs. Now, every morning when I rise I go at once into the garden at four o'clock and make a business of slaughtering them till half past five, when I stop for breakfast. If the day is pleasant they are all hidden by that time, for they dread so the touch of the sun. But in the hoary morning dew they delight. This is the hardest part of my gardening, and I rejoice that not one person in a thousand has this plague of slugs to fight. It is so difficult to destroy them; to see their countless legions and feel so helpless before their numbers, to find one's most precious favorites nibbled and ragged, and everything threatened with destruction is a trial indeed. I carry a large pepper-box filled with air-slaked lime and shake it over them everywhere. They are so small this year that it destroys them; they turn milky and miserably perish, but the next morn-ing there are just as many more to take their places. Still I patiently persevere, carefully washing off the lime, so anxious lest it should harm the plants, and killing by hand all the larger monsters.

In that most charming old book, Gilbert White's "Natural History of Selborne," I find he speaks of these arch enemies of mine as "un-noticed myriads of small shell-less snails called slugs, which silently and imperceptibly make amazing havoc in field and garden;" adding in a note, " Farmer Young of Norton Farm says that this spring (1777) about four acres of his wheat in one field were entirely destroyed by the slugs, which swarmed on the blades of corn and devoured it as fast as it sprung."

Poor Farmer Young! I deeply sympathize with him and his long buried trouble!

Again White says: " The shell-less snails called slugs are in motion all winter in mild weather and commit great depredations on garden plants, and much injure the green wheat."

There was a happy time when such a thing as a slug was unknown on my island, and I well re-member the first that were brought here among some Moonflowers that were imported from a dis-tant green-house. I saw them adhering to the outside of the flower-pots and did not kill them, never dreaming what powers of evil they would become!

25th. Every day the garden grows more inter-esting, more fascinating. Buds full of promise show themselves on the single Dahlias whose seeds were only planted in February; on the Rose Campions, the perennial kind, on the tall white Lilies. The Hollyhocks are thick with buds, and rich spikes head all the boughs of the Larkspurs, and as for the Roses, they are simply wonderful. The Tea Roses are loaded with buds; on one of the Polyanthas that lived all winter in the ground

I counted fifty-two, and it is a tiny bush not more than a foot high.   The dear old Sweet Rocket is blossoming in every corner, sending up its grateful perfume.   Now come days of great anxiety about the Margaret Carnations that I have so loved and watched and tended since the first of March.   They were splendid plants, full of health and strength and all ready to bloom.   Alas, I saw, a day or two ago, the leaves turning yellow.   I knew too well what that meant.   There was but one thing to do.   Down on my knees I went this morning, and bringing my face close to the ground, began pulling apart the central shoot in each plant, where the sickly color hung its flag of distress for a signal.   Down, down a cruel length, into the very heart and core of each precious stem I tore my reluctant way to find that abomination of which I was in search, namely, a short fat lively white worm; for him I probed and brought him up on the point of a pin, and having a small quantity of alcohol at hand for the purpose, dropped him into it forthwith, for instant and complete destruction.   Over forty of these beasts did I destroy, and left the tattered Pinks to rest and recover, if they could, poor things, after such a terrible experience!   These worms seem made for all fragrant Pinks; as far as my experience goes they never attack anything else.   How in the world, I wonder, do they know where the Carnations are planted and when to come for them? Such a scene of devastation as is my pretty bed of Pinks of which I was so proud, dwarfed and yellow, with their gnawed-off leaves strewn about

all over the ground! But they will put out side
shoots and patiently strive to fulfill heaven's intent for them, of which they are conscious from
the least root-tip to the end of every battered leaf.
There is something pathetic as well as wonderful
in the way in which these growing things of almost all kinds meet disaster and discouragement.
Should they suffer misfortune like this, — the lop-
ping of a limb, or the losing of buds, or any sap-
ping of their vitality, — if the cause is removed,
they will try so hard to repair damages, send out
new shoots, make strenuous efforts to recover the
lost ground, and still perfect blossom and fruit as
nature meant they should. There is a lesson to
be learned of them on which I have often pondered.

June 3d. This has been an exciting day, for the
Water Lilies I sent for a week ago came in a mysterious damp box across the ocean foam! I had
made their tubs all ready for them, putting in the
bottom of each the " well-rotted manure," and over
this rich earth and sand mixed in proper propor-
tions. These tubs, or rather large, tall butter firkins,
stood ready in their places along the sunniest and
most sheltered bed in the garden. Oh, the pleasure of opening that box and finding each unfamiliar treasure packed so carefully in wet moss,
each folded in oiled paper to keep it moist, and
each labeled with its fascinating name! The great
pink Lotus of Egypt, the purple Lily of Zanzibar, and the red one of the same sort, the golden
Chromatella, the pure white African variety and
the smaller native white one, the yellow Water

Poppy and the little exquisite plant called Parrot's Feather, that creeps all about over the water and has the wonderful living, metallic green of the plumage of the handsome green parrots. These, with the flourishing Water Hyacinth I already had growing in its tub on the steps, and the bright pink Cape Cod Lily, make ten tubs of water plants, — a most breathlessly interesting family! And I must not forget another tub of seedling Water-Lilies that I am watching with the most intense interest also. It took most of the long, happy day to plant all these in the rich wet mud and settle them in their comfortable quarters. I laid some horseshoes I had picked up at different times, and saved, round the roots to hold them down temporarily, while I gently flooded the tubs with water and rejoiced to see the lovely leaves float out on the surface fresh as if they were at home. Then I sifted clean beach sand over the earth about them, to the depth of an inch or more, to hold the soil down and keep the water clear, and all was done. What delight to look forward to the watching and tending of these new friends! I find myself wondering what enemy will attack these, for surely something has been made for their destruction, which I must fight! There is not a growing thing in the garden that has not its enemies and destroyers, fortunate if it has only one. Just at this time there is a rampant little snuff-colored spider which comes in from the grass and fastens upon tender growths in the borders about the house, covering the succulent leaves and stems of Wild Cucumbers and Morn-

ing-glories, and even Nasturtiums and Cornflowers, so thickly that the plant is not to be seen at
all for them; they are like a brown glove over
every leaf, and they suck every drop of sap out of
the plant, leaving it perfectly white. They are
fatal on the Sweet Peas, of which they are especially fond. No poison known to me has the
slightest effect on them; nothing but water turned
on with the hose in floods disturbs them. This
washes them away for the time being. It has to
be repeated, however, many times a day, for they
recover from their drenching and return to their
work of devastation with renewed vigor. Fortunately these do not, like the slugs, last forever;
they are gone in less than six weeks; but they
keep me busy indeed while they stay.

I am obliged to spend a good deal of time just
now hunting and destroying different bugs and
worms and so forth. The blue-green aphis appears on certain precious Honeysuckle buds, and
must be vigorously syringed with fir-tree oil before
he gets a foothold and spreads his hideous legions
everywhere. Also the lively worm that ties the
Rose leaves together and gobbles them up and
hides in a web within them, that I may find and
crush him; and the white thrip which calls for
hellebore, on the under side of them, and many
more, must be attended to before they wax strong
and bold in their villainy and defy me. A curious
plague, if I may call it so, has come upon the little
garden, in the shape of the delicious edible mushrooms, Coprinus Comatus, which come up all over
the place and with slow strength heave the

ground and my flowers into heaps, thrusting
handsome long ivory-white, umbrella-shaped heads
on stems a foot long, up high above and over
most things in the beds.   But these are eaten as
soon as they appear, and are not such a very
great trial, though I would rather they left my
dear flowers undisturbed.

MUCH thought should be given to the garden's arrangement with regard to economy of room, where one has but a small space to devote to it. And where one is unfamiliar with the habits of growth of the various plants that are to people it, a difficulty arises in making them effective and so disposing them that they shall not interfere with each other. For instance, in most cases tall plants should be put back against walls and fences and so forth, with the lower-growing varieties in the foreground. If one were to plant Verbenas and Venidium among Sunflowers and Hollyhocks, or even among Carnation Poppies and Cornflowers, Verbenas and Venidium would not be visible, for their habit is to creep close to the ground, and the tall growths would completely hide and most likely exterminate them, by shutting from them the sun and air without which they cannot live. These low, creeping plants are, however, very useful when one is planning for a succession of flowers. I plant Pansies, Verbenas, Drummond's Phlox, and so forth, among my Pinks and Wall-flowers and others of like compact habit, so that, when the higher slender plants have done blossoming, the others, which seldom cease flowering till frost, may still clothe the ground with color and beauty. Of course it goes without saying that climbing Vines should not be set where there is nothing upon which they may climb. Indeed that would be simple cruelty — nothing more nor less. Everything that needs it should be given a support without fail — all the myriad lovely Vines that one may have with so little trouble, and which seem to have been made to wreathe the dwellings of men with freshness and beauty and grace. The long list of varieties of flowering Clematis, so many shapes and colors, the numerous Honeysuckles, the Wistaria, Passion - flowers, Morning-glories, Hops, the Dutchman's Pipe, the Cobœas, Woodbine, and many others, not counting Sweet Peas and Nasturtiums, — these last among the most beautiful and decorative of all, — every one is twice as valuable if given the support it demands. In the case of Nasturtiums, however, which seem with endless good-nature ready to adapt themselves to any conditions of existence, except, perhaps, being expected to live in a swamp, it is not so important that they should have something upon which to climb. A very good way is to put them near a rock one wishes to have covered, or to let them run down a bank upon which nothing else cares to grow. They will clothe such places with wild and beautiful luxuriance of green leaves and glowing flowers.

It seems strange to write a book about a little garden only fifty feet long by fifteen wide! But then, as a friend pleasantly remarked to me, " it extends upward," and what it lacks in area is more than compensated by the large joy that grows out of it and its uplifting and refreshment of " the Spirit of Man."

I have made a plan of this minute domain to show how it may be possible to accomplish much within such narrow compass, and also to give an idea of an advantageous method of grouping in a space so confined. I have not room to experiment with rockworks and ribbon-borders and the like, nor should I do it even if I had all the room in the world. For mine is just a little old-fashioned garden where the flowers come together to praise the Lord and teach all who look upon them to do likewise.

All through the months of April and May, when the weather is not simply impossible, I am at work in it, and also through most of June. It is wonderful how much work one can find to do in so tiny a plot of ground. But in the latter weeks of June there comes a time when I can begin to take breath and rest a little from these difficult yet pleasant labors; an interval when I may take time to consider, a morning when I may seek the hammock in the shady piazza, and, looking across my happy flower beds, let the sweet day sink deep into my heart. From the flower beds I look over the island slopes to the sea, and realize it all, — the rapture of growth, the delicious shades of green that clothe the ground, Wild

Rose, Bayberry, Spirea, Shadbush, Elder, and many more. How beautiful they are, these grassy, rocky slopes shelving gradually to the sea, with here and there a mass of tall, blossoming grass softly swaying in the warm wind against the peaceful, pale blue water! Among the grass a few ghostly dandelion tops yet linger, with now and then a belated golden flower. How lovely is the delicacy of the white bleached rocks, the little spaces of shallow soil exquisite with vivid crimson Sorrel, or pearly with the brave Eyebright, all against the soft color of the sea. What harmony of movement in all these radiant growths just stirred by the gentle air! Here and there a stout little bough of Chokecherry, with clustered white blossoms tipped with pink, springing from a cleft in the rock, lights up in sunshine, its pink more glowing for the turquoise background of the ocean. How hot the sun blazes! The Blue-eyed Grass is quite faint and drooping in the rich turf, but the yellow Crowfoot shines strong and steady; no sunshine is too bright for it. In the garden the tall Jacqueminot Rosebushes gather power from the great warmth and light, and hold out their thick buds to absorb it and fold its splendor in their inmost hearts. One or two of the heaviest buds begin to loosen their crimson velvet petals and shed their delicious perfume on the air. The Oriental Poppy glories in the heat. Among its buds, thrust upward like solid green apples, one has burst into burning flame, each of its broad fiery petals as large as the whole inside of my hand. In the Iceland Poppy bed the ardent light

has wooed a graceful company of drooping buds
to blow, and their cups of delicate fire, orange and
yellow, sway lightly on stems as slender as grass.
In sheltered corners the Forget-me-not spreads its
cool, heaven-blue clusters; by the fence "the Larkspurs listen" while they wait; the large purple
Pansies shrink and turn from the too brilliant gaze
of the sun.   Rose Campions, Tea Roses, Mignonette, Marigolds, Coreopsis, the rows of Sweet Peas,
the broad-leaved Hollyhocks and the rest, rejoice
and grow visibly with every moment of the glorious day.   Clematis and Honeysuckle almost seem
to hurry, Nasturtiums reach their shield-like leaves
and wind the stems thereof round any and every
stick and string they can touch by which to lift
themselves, here and there showing their first
glowing flowers, and climbing eagerly.   The long
large buds of the white Clematis, the earliest of
all, are swelling visibly before my eyes, and the
buds of the early June Honeysuckle are reddening
at the end of every spray.   In one corner a tall
purple Columbine hangs its myriad clustered
bells ; each flower has six shell-like whorls set in a
circle, colored like rich amethysts and lined with
lustrous silver, white as frost.   Cornflowers like
living sparks of exquisite color, rose and azure,
white and purple, twinkle all over the place, and
the heavenly procession begins in good earnest.
The Grapevine smooths out its young leaves, —
they are woolly and crimson ; the wind blows and
shows me their grayish-white under surfaces.   I
think of Browning's tender song, the verse, —

" The leaf buds on the vine are woolly,
    I noticed that to-day,
One day more bursts them open fully,
    You know the red turns gray."

The Echinocystus plants that have sprung in thick ranks along the edge of the beds against the piazza are fairly storming up the trellis, having sown themselves in the autumn; they have just really begun to take firm hold, and are climbing hand over hand, as sailors do, with their strong green tendrils stretching out like arms and hands to right and left, laying hold of every available thing by which to cling and spring upward to the very eaves. There in August they form a closely woven curtain of lush, light green, overhung with large, loose clusters of starry white flowers having a pure, delicious fragrance like honey and the wax of the comb.

Now come the most perfect days of the year, blue days, hot on the continent, but heavenly here, where the cool breeze breathes round the islands from the great expanse of whispering water. Delightful it is to lie here and rest and realize all this beauty and rejoice in all its joy! The distant coast-line is dim in soft mirage.

" Half lost in the liquid azure bloom of a crescent of sea,
    The silent, sapphire-spangled, marriage-ring of the land."

It lies so lovely, far away! At its edge the water is glassy calm, the houses and large, glimmering piles of buildings along its whole length show white in the hot haze; in the offing the far-off sails are half lost in this shimmering veil;

farther out there is a soft wind blowing; little fishing-boats with their sails furled lie at anchor between us and the land, faintly outlined against the delicate tone of the water. All is so still! I hear a bee go blundering into the Bachelor's Buttons that hold up their flowers to the sun like small, compact yellow Roses. Suddenly comes a gush of the song-sparrow's music, but father martin sits at his door very quiet; it is too hot on the red roof of his little house, so he sits at its portal and meditates while his small wife broods within, only now and then from his pretty throat pours a low ripple of sound, melodiously content. I am conscious of the sandpiper calling and the full tide murmuring, and I, too, am content.

Outside the garden fence it is as if the flowers had broken their bounds and were rushing down the sloping bank in a torrent of yellow, where the early Artemisias and Eschscholtzias are hastening into bloom, overflowing in a flood of gold that, lightly stirred by every breeze, sends a satin shimmer to the sun. Eschscholtzia — it is an ugly name for a most lovely flower. California Poppy is much better. Down into the sweet plot I go and gather a few of these, bringing them to my little table and sitting down before them the better to admire and adore their beauty. In the slender green glass in which I put them they stand clothed in their delicate splendor. One blossom I take in a loving hand the more closely to examine it, and it breathes a glory of color into sense and spirit which is enough to kindle the dullest imagination. The stems and fine thread-like leaves are

smooth and cool gray-green, as if to temper the
fire of the blossoms, which are smooth also, un-
like almost all other Poppies, that are crumpled
past endurance in their close green buds, and
make one feel as if they could not wait to break
out of the calyx and loosen their petals to the
sun, to be soothed into even tranquillity of beauty
by the touches of the air.   Every cool gray-green
leaf is tipped with a tiny line of red, every flower-
bud wears a little pale-green pointed cap like an
elf, and in the early morning, when the bud is
ready to blow, it pushes off the pretty cap and unfolds all its loveliness to the sun.   Nothing could
be more picturesque than this fairy cap, and nothing more charming than to watch the blossom
push it off and spread its yellow petals, slowly
rounding to the perfect cup.   As I hold the flower
in my hand and think of trying to describe it, I
realize how poor a creature I am, how impotent
are words in the presence of such perfection.   It
is held upright upon a straight and polished
stem, its petals curving upward and outward into
the cup of light, pure gold with a lustrous satin
sheen ; a rich orange is painted on the gold, drawn
in infinitely fine lines to a point in the centre of
the edge of each petal, so that the effect is that
of a diamond of flame in a cup of gold.   It is not
enough that the powdery anthers are orange bordered with gold ; they are whirled about the very
heart of the flower like a revolving Catherine-
wheel of fire.   In the centre of the anthers is a
shining point of warm sea-green, a last, consummate touch which makes the beauty of the blos-

som supreme. Another has the orange suffused through the gold evenly, almost to the outer edges of the petals, which are left in bright, light yellow with a dazzling effect. Turning the flower and looking at it from the outside, it has no calyx, but the petals spring from a simple pale-green disk, which must needs be edged with sea-shell pink for the glory of God! The fresh splendor of this flower no tongue nor pen nor brush of mortal man can fitly represent.

Who indeed shall adequately describe any one, the simplest even, of these radiant beings? Day after day, as I watch them appear, one variety after another, in such endless changes of delicate beauty, I can but marvel ever more and more at the exhaustless power of the great Inventor. Must He not enjoy the work of His hands, the manifold perfection of these His matchless creations? Who can behold the unfolding of each new spring and all its blossoms without feeling the renewal of " God's ancient rapture," of which Browning speaks in " Paracelsus "? In that immortal rapture, I, another of his creatures, less obedient in fulfilling His laws of beauty than are these lovely beings, do humbly share, reflecting it with all the powers of my spirit and rejoicing in His work with an exceeding joy.

As the days go on toward July, the earth becomes dry and all the flowers begin to thirst for moisture. Then from the hillside, some warm, still evening, the sweet rain-song of the robin echoes clear, and next day we wake to a dim morning; soft flecks of cloud bar the sun's way, fleecy vapors steal across the sky, the southwest wind blows lightly, rippling the water into little waves that murmur melodiously as they kiss the shore. In this warm gray, brooding light I am reminded of Tennyson's subtle description of such a daybreak : —

"When the first low matin chirp hath grown
Full quire, and morning driven her plough of pearl
Far furrowing into light the mounded rack,
Beyond the fair green field and eastern sea."

Through the early hours of the day the mottled, pearly clouds keep their shape, with delicious open spaces of tempered blue between ; by and by the sky's tender fleece is half shadowed, toward noon it melts into loose mists. Color everywhere tells against these pellucid grays, — the gold of Lemon Lilies, the flame of Iceland Poppies, all the sweet tints of every blossom. Presently the happy rain begins to fall, so soft, so warm, so peaceful, the very sound of it is a pleasure ; every leaf in the patient garden, which has waited for the shower so long, spreads itself wide to catch each crystal drop and treasure its deep refreshment. All day it rains ; at night the melody lulls us to sleep as it patters on the roof. In the night the wind changes, and next day brings a northeast storm again with a wild wind, but from this the little flower plot is well protected, and I rejoice in the thorough watering deep down among their roots which is doing all the plants unmeasured good. Two, perhaps three days, it lasts, the gale blowing till there is such contention of winds and waves about the little isle as to make a ceaseless roaring of wild breakers round its shores. When at last the tempest wears itself out, what delight there is in the great tranquillity that follows it, what music in the soft, far murmurs of ceasing strife in air and ocean, spent wrath that seems to breathe yet in an undertone, half sullen, half relenting, while the broad yellow light that lies over sea and rocks in stillness, like a quiet smile, promises a heavenly day on the morrow.

Then, with what fresh wealth of color and perfume the garden will meet the resplendent sunrise! Every moment it grows more and more beautiful. I think for wondrous variety, for certain picturesque qualities, for color and form and a subtle mystery of character, Poppies seem, on the whole, the most satisfactory flowers among the annuals. There is absolutely no limit to their variety of color. They are the tenderest lilac, the deepest crimson, richest scarlet, white with softest suffusion of rose; all shades of rose, clear light pink with sea-green centre, the anthers in a golden halo about it; black and fire-color; red that is deepened to black, with gray reflections; cherry-color, with a cross of creamy white at the bottom of the cup, and round its central altar of ineffable golden green again the halo of yellow anthers; purple, with rich splashes of a deeper shade of the same color, with grayish white rays about the centre; all shades of lavender and lilac; exquisite smoke-color, in some cases delicately touched and freaked with red; some pure light gray, some of these gray ones edged with crimson or scarlet; there are all tints of mauve. To tell all the combinations of their wonderful hues, or even half, would be quite impossible, from the simple transparent scarlet bell of the wild Poppy to the marvelous pure white, the wonder of which no tongue can tell. Oh, these white Poppies, some with petals more delicate than the finest tissue paper, with centres of bright gold, some of thicker quality, large, shell-like petals, almost ribbed in their effect, their green knob in the middle like a boss upon a shield, rayed about with beautiful grayish yellow stamens, as in the kind called the Bride. Others — they call this kind the Snowdrift — have thick double flowers, deeply cut and fringed at the edges, the most opaque white, and full of exquisite shadows. Then there are the Icelanders, which Lieutenant Peary found making gay the frosty fields of Greenland, in buttercup-yellow and orange and white; the great Orientals, gorgeous beyond expression; the immense single white California variety. I could not begin to name them all in the longest summer's day! The Thorn Poppy, Argemone, is a fascinating variety, most quaint in method of growth and most decorative. As for the Shirleys, they are children of the dawn, and inherit all its delicate, vivid, delicious suffusions of rose-color in every conceivable shade. Of the Poppy one of the great masters of English prose discourses in this wise. Speaking of the common wild Poppy of the English fields, which grows broadcast also over most of Europe, he says: " The splendor of it is proud, almost insolently so," which immediately brings to mind Browning's lines in " Sordello," —

" The Poppy's red effrontery,
Till autumn spoils its fleering quite with rain,
And portionless, a dry, brown, rattling crane
Protrudes."

Papaver Rhœas is the common wild scarlet Poppy that both these writers describe. John Ruskin says : " I have in my hand a small red Poppy which I gathered on Whit Sunday in the palace of the Cæsars. It is an intensely simple, intensely floral flower. All silk and flame, a scarlet cup, perfect edged all round, seen among the wild grass far away like a burning coal fallen from Heaven's altars. You cannot have a more complete, a more stainless type of flower absolute ; inside and outside, all flower. No sparing of color anywhere, no outside coarsenesses, no interior secrecies, open as the sunshine that creates it; fine finished on both sides, down to the extremest point of insertion on its narrow stalk, and robed in the purple of the Cæsars. . . .

" Literally so. That Poppy scarlet, so far as could be painted by mortal hand, for mortal king, stays yet, against the sun and wind and rain, on the walls of the house of Augustus, a hundred yards from the spot where I gathered the weed of its desolation. . . . The flower in my hand is a poverty *stricken* Poppy, I was going to write, poverty *strengthened* Poppy, I mean. On richer ground it would have gushed into flaunting breadth of untenable purple ; flapped its inconsistent scarlet vaguely to the wind ; dropped the pride of its petals over my hand in an hour after I gathered it. But this little rough-bred thing . . .

is as bright and strong to-day as yesterday. . . . What outline its petals really have is little shown in their crumpled fluttering, but that very crumpling arises from a fine floral character which we do not enough value in them. We usually think of a Poppy as a coarse flower; but it is the most transparent and delicate of all the blossoms of the field. The rest, nearly all of them, depend on the texture of their surfaces for color. But the Poppy is painted glass; it never glows so brightly as when the sun shines through it. Wherever it is seen, against the light or with the light, always it is a flame, and warms the wind like a blown ruby. . . . Gather a green Poppy bud, just when it shows the scarlet line at its side, break it open and unpack the Poppy. The whole flower is there complete in size and color, its stamens full grown, but all packed so closely that the fine silk of the petals is crushed into a million of wrinkles. When the flower opens, it seems a relief from torture; the two imprisoning green leaves are shaken to the ground, the aggrieved corolla smooths itself in the sun and comforts itself as best it can, but remains crushed and hurt to the end of its days."

I know of no flower that has so many charming tricks and manners, none with a method of growth more picturesque and fascinating. The stalks often take a curve, a twist from some current of air or some impediment, and the fine stems will turn and bend in all sorts of graceful ways, but the bud is always held erect when the time comes for it to blossom. Ruskin quotes

Lindley's definition of what constitutes a Poppy, which he thinks "might stand." This is it: "A Poppy is a flower which has either four or six petals, and two or more treasuries united in one, containing a milky, stupefying fluid in its stalks and leaves, and always throwing away its calyx when it blossoms."

I muse over their seed-pods, those supremely graceful urns that are wrought with such matchless elegance of shape, and think what strange power they hold within. Sleep is there, and Death his brother, imprisoned in those mystic sealed cups. There is a hint of their mystery in their shape of sombre beauty, but never a suggestion in the fluttering blossom; it is the gayest flower that blows. In the more delicate varieties the stalks are so slender, yet so strong, like fine grass stems, when you examine them you wonder how they hold even the light weight of the flower so firmly and proudly erect. They are clothed with the finest of fine hairs up and down the stalks, and over the green calyx, especially in the Iceland varieties, where these hairs are of a lovely red-brown color and add much to their beauty.

It is plain to see, as one gazes over the Poppy beds on some sweet evening at sunset, what buds will bloom in the joy of next morning's first sunbeams, for these will be lifting themselves heavenward, slowly and silently, but surely. To stand by the beds at sunrise and see the flowers awake is a heavenly delight. As the first long, low rays of the sun strike the buds, you know they feel the signal! A light air stirs among them; you lift your eyes, perhaps to look at a rosy cloud or follow the flight of a caroling bird, and when you look back again, lo! the calyx has fallen from the largest bud and lies on the ground, two half transparent, light green shells, leaving the flower petals wrinkled in a thousand folds, just released from their close pressure. A moment more and they are unclosing before your eyes. They flutter out on the gentle breeze like silken banners to the sun, and such a color! The orange of the Iceland Poppy is the most ineffable color; it "warms the wind" indeed! I know no tint like it; it is orange dashed with carmine, most like the reddest coals of an intensely burning fire. Look at this exquisite cup: the wind has blown nearly smooth the crinkled petals; these, where they meet in the centre, melt into a delicate greenish yellow. In the heart of the blossom rises a round green altar, its sides penciled with nine black lines, and a nine-rayed star of yellow velvet clasps the flat, pure green top. From the base of this altar springs the wreath of stamens and anthers; the inner circle of these is generally white, the outer yellow, and all held high and clear within the cup. The radiant effect of this arrangement against the living red cannot be told.

The Californias put out their clean, polished, pointed buds straight up to the sun from the first, but all the others have this fashion of drooping theirs till the evening before they blow. There is a kind of triumph in the way they do this, lifting their treasured splendor yet safe within its clasping calyx to be ready to meet the first beams of the day.

The Orientals are glorious, even in the victorious family of Poppies. Ruskin has a chapter on " The Rending of Leaves." I always think of it when I see the large, hairy, rich green leaves of this variety, which are deeply " rent," almost the whole width of the leaf to the midrib. These leaves grow somewhat after the fashion of a Dandelion, spreading several feet in all directions from the centre, which sends up in June immense flower-stalks crowned with heavy apple-like buds, that elongate as they increase in size, till some morning the thick calyx breaks and falls, and the great scarlet flags of the flower unfold. There is a kind of angry brilliance about it, a sombre and startling magnificence. Its lârge petals are splashed near the base with broad, irregular spots of black-purple, as if they had been struck with a brush full of color. The seed-pod, rising fully an inch high in the centre, is of a luminous, indescribable shade of green, and folded over its top, a third of its height, is a cap of rich lavender, laid down in points evenly about the crown. On the centre of this is a little knob of deep purple velvet, from which eleven rays of the same color curve over the top and into each point of the lavender cap. And round this wonderful seed-pod, with its wealth of elaborate ornament, is a thick girdle of stamens half an inch deep, with row upon row and circle within circle of anthers covered with dust of splendid dusky purple, and held each upon a slender thread of deeper purple still. It is simply superb, and when the great bush is ablaze with these flowers it is indeed a conflagration of color. " The fire-engines always turn out when my Orientals blaze up on the hillside," writes a flower-loving friend to me. No garden should be without these, for they flourish with the least care, are perfectly hardy, and never fail to blossom generously.

HAT every plant should select only its own colors and forms from the great laboratory of Nature has always seemed to me a very wonderful thing. Each plant takes from its surroundings just those qualities which will produce its own especial characteristics and no others, never hesitating and never making a mistake. For instance, the California Poppies, if left to themselves, will take yellow of many resplendent shades for their color, and never vary their cool, gray-green, red-tipped foliage; the Peacock Poppy will be always scarlet-crimson, with a black spot rimmed with white in every petal; the Corn Poppy will be always clear scarlet; the Bride a miracle of lustrous white, and so on. Runge, a noted chemist, says: "A plant is a great chemist: it distinguishes and separates substances more definitely and accurately than man can, with all his skill, his intelligence, and his appliances. . . . The little Daisy, which has painted its ' wee crimson-tipped flowers,' puts the chemist and scientific man to shame, for it has produced its leaf and stem and flowers, and has dyed these with their bright colors from materials which he can never change with all his arts."

By what power do they know how to select each its own hue and shape, when earth and air hold all the tints and forms that the Creator has invented? The subtle knowledge of plants, instinct perhaps would be a better word, is astonishing. If you dig a hole in the ground and put into it a Rosebush, filling one side of the hole with rich earth and the other with poor soil, every root of that Rosebush will leave the poor half to inhabit the rich and nourishing portion. That is a matter of course, but the instinct of the Rose is something to think about, nevertheless.

Some one has said, speaking of a tree, " What an immense amount of vitally organized material has been here gathered together! It is God's own architecture! This mass of vegetable matter is only earth and air that have undergone transmutation. The material alike of wandering zephyrs and rushing storms, of gently descending night-dews and angry thunder-showers has been *here, on this spot*, metamorphosed."

And I should add that into this piece of architecture God has breathed a vital spark, almost a mind, so remarkable is the intelligent action often manifested in many plants and trees.

A famous Frenchman, Camille Flammarion, says: " I know a maple-tree which was dying on the ruins of an old wall, a few feet from good rich earth (the soil in a ditch), and which in despair threw out a venturesome root, reached the coveted earth, buried itself there, and gained a solid footing, so that by degrees, although a motionless thing, it changed its place, let its original roots die, and lived resuscitated upon the organ that had set it free. I have known elms which were going to eat up the soil of a fertile field, whose food had been cut off from them by a wide ditch, and who, therefore, determined to make their uncut roots pass under the ditch. They succeeded, and returned to their regular food, much to the cultivator's astonishment. I know an heroic Jasmine which went eight times through a board which kept the light away from it, and which a teasing observer would put back in the shade, hoping so to wear out the flower's energy, but he did not succeed."

This happened in France, but here in New England I myself know of a great Wistaria which grew over one side of a fine old house in an enchanting garden, and which did something quite as wonderful. It was a triumph of a vine! The butt or stump, where it emerged from the ground, was a foot in diameter, and its branches covered one side of the house, a space of thirty feet by thirty feet. So large a vine required a great deal of water, so it sent its roots down eight feet under the foundation of the house, passed along under the brick floor of the dairy, a distance of fifteen feet, making a solid mat of roots under the whole floor, reached the well and went straight through the cracks and crevices of its stone wall to the desired moisture. An elm root in the same

garden went sixty feet or more under the foundation of the house to that same well.

To quote another writer who has carefully ob-
served these things: "Plants have to the full
extent of their necessities a power of observation,
of discrimination in the selection of their food, a
knowledge of where it is to be found, and the
power to a considerable extent to obtain it. For
instance, if some animal's remains are buried in
the garden, say twenty feet from the grapevine,
the vine will know it, and the underground part
of the vine will at once change its course and
make a direct march for this new storehouse of
food, and upon reaching it will throw out an in-
credible number of roots for its consumption.
. . . A weeping willow was planted in a dry,
gravelly soil on the south side of a house, a
situation in every respect unsuited to this tree,
which delights in a heavy moist soil; the result
was a slow, stunted growth. After a few years in
which it barely lived, it surprised its owner by a
vigorous growth which was as astonishing as
pleasing, and the cause was looked for. It was
found the roots in search of food had traveled
under the house a distance of some thirty feet to
the well, where they took a downward course till
they reached the water that furnished the moisture which is essential to the growth of this tree.

"The movements of the squash vine when
pressed by hunger or thirst are truly wonderful.
During a severe drought if you place a basin of
water at night, say two feet to the left or the
right of a strong vine, in the morning it will be

found bathing in the basin! Is not this an indication of thought in the vine? Does it not indicate a knowledge in the vine analogous to human understanding? . . . There must be some agent employed to bring the vine to the fountain. . . .

"The more we study plant life the more we become convinced that life is a unit, varying in form only, not in principle. Everything capable of reproduction, growth, and development is governed by the same law, and each is but a part of the unit we term life."

Again to quote the famous Frenchman: "When I breathe the perfume of a Rose," he says, "when I admire the beauty of form, the grace of this flower in its freshly opening bloom, what strikes me most is the work of that hidden, unknown, mysterious force which rules over the plant's life and can direct it in the maintenance of its existence, which chooses the proper molecules of air, water, and earth for its nourishment, and which knows, above all, how to assimilate these molecules and group them so delicately as to form this graceful stem, these dainty green leaves, these soft pink petals, these exquisite tints and delicious fragrance. . . .

"This mysterious force is the animating principle of the plant. Put a Lily seed, an acorn, a grain of wheat, and a peach-stone side by side in the ground, each germ will build up its own organism and no other. . . .

"A plant breathes, drinks, eats, selects, refuses, seeks, works, lives, acts, according to its instincts. One does like a charm, another pines, a third is nervous and agitated.   The Sensitive Plant shivers and droops its leaves at the slightest touch."

Climbing plants show often a surprising degree of intelligence, reaching out for support as if they had eyes to see.   I have known a vine whose head was aimlessly waving in the wind, with nothing near it to which it might cling, turn deliberately round in an opposite direction to that in which it had been growing and seize a line I had stretched for it to grasp, without any help outside itself, and within the space of an hour's time.   By manifold ways they cling and climb, many by winding their stems round and round strings or sticks or wires, or whatever is given them, as do the Morning-glories, Hop, Honeysuckle, Wistarias, and many others; but Sweet Peas, Cobœa, and so forth, put out a delicate tendril at the end of each leaf, or rather group of leaves.   Nasturtiums, Clematis, and others take a turn with their leaf-stems round anything that comes in their way, and so lift and hold themselves securely, and the Echinocystus or Wild Cucumber has a system of tendrils strong as iron and elastic as India-rubber.   It is most interesting to observe them all and ponder on their different charming ways and habits, to help them if they need it, and to sympathize with all their experiences.   As I work among my flowers, I find myself talking to them, reasoning and remonstrating with them, and adoring them as if they were human beings.   Much laughter I provoke among my friends by so doing, but that is of no consequence.   We are on such good terms, my flowers and I !

Altogether lovely they are out of doors, but I plant and tend them always with the thought of the joy they will be within the house also. I know well what Emerson means when he asks,

" Hast thou named all the birds without a gun ?
Loved the wood Rose and left it on its stalk ? "

and if I gather this or any other wild-flower I do it with such reverent love that even he would be satisfied. No one knows better and deplores more deeply than I the wholesale destruction, wanton and cruel, which goes on among our wild-flowers every year; but to bring a few indoors for purposes of study and fuller appreciation is another and a desirable thing. For the wild Rose is but partially learned when one pauses a moment in passing to admire the sweet surprise of its beauty as it suddenly smiles up from the roadside. It cannot be learned in a single glance, nor, indeed, in many glances : it must be carefully considered and lovingly meditated upon before it yields all the marvel of its delicate glory to your intelligence. " Consider the Lilies," said the Master. Truly, there is no more prayerful business than this "consideration" of all the flowers that grow.

And in the garden they are planted especially to feast the souls that hunger for beauty, and within doors as well as without they " delight the spirit of man." Opening out on the long piazza over the flower beds, and extending almost its whole length, runs the large, light, airy room where a group of happy people gather to pass the

swiftly flying summers here at the Isles of Shoals.
This room is made first for music; on the polished
floor is no carpet to muffle sound, only a few rugs
here and there, like patches of warm green moss
on the pine-needle color given by the polish to
the natural hue of the wood. There are no heavy
draperies to muffle the windows, nothing to absorb the sound. The piano stands midway at
one side; there are couches, sofas with pillows
of many shades of dull, rich color, but mostly of
warm shades of green. There are low bookcases
round the walls, the books screened by short cur-
tains of pleasant olive-green; the high walls to
the ceiling are covered with pictures, and flowers
are everywhere. The shelves of the tall mantel
are splendid with massed Nasturtiums like a blazing torch, beginning with the palest yellow, almost
white, and piled through every deepening shade
of gold, orange, scarlet, crimson, to the blackest
red; all along the tops of the low bookcases burn
the fires of Marigolds, Coreopsis, large flowers of
the velvet single Dahlias in yellow, flame, and
scarlet of many shades, masses of pure gold summer Chrysanthemums, and many more, — all here
and there interspersed with blossoming grasses
for a touch of ethereal green. On one low bookcase are Shirley Poppies in a roseate cloud. And
here let me say that the secret of keeping Poppies
in the house two whole days without fading is
this: they must be gathered early, before the dew
has dried, in the morning. I go forth between
five and six o'clock to cut them while yet their
gray-green leaves are hoary with dew, taking a tall

slender pitcher or bottle of water with me into the garden, and as I cut each stem dropping the flower at once into it, so that the stem is covered nearly its whole length with water; and so on till the pitcher is full. Gathered in this way, they have no opportunity to lose their freshness, indeed, the exquisite creatures hardly know they have been gathered at all. When I have all I need, I begin on the left end of this bookcase, which most felicitously fronts the light, and into the glasses put the radiant blossoms with an infinite enjoyment of the work. The glasses (thirty-two in all) themselves are beautiful: nearly all are white, clear and pure, with a few pale green and paler rose and delicate blue, one or two of richer pink, all brilliantly clear and filled with absolutely colorless water, through which the stems show their slender green lengths. Into the glasses at this end on the left I put first the dazzling white single Poppy, the Bride, to lead the sweet procession, — a marvelous blossom, whose pure white is half transparent, with its central altar of ineffable green and gold. A few of these first, then a dozen or more of delicate tissue-paper-like blossoms of snow in still another variety (with petals so thin that a bright color behind them shows through their filmy texture); then the double kind called Snowdrift, which being double makes a deeper body of whiteness flecked with softest shadow. Then I begin with the palest rose tints, placing them next, and slightly mingling a few with the last white ones, — a rose tint delicate as the palm of a baby's hand; then the

next, with a faint suffusion of a blush, and go on
to the next shade, still very delicate, not deeper
than the soft hue on the lips of the great whelk
shells in southern seas; then the damask rose
color and all tints of tender pink, then the deeper
tones to clear, rich cherry, and on to glowing
crimson, through a mass of this to burning
maroon.

The flowers are of all heights (the stems of
different lengths), and, though massed, are in
broken and irregular ranks, the tallest standing
a little over two feet high. But there is no crush-
ing or crowding. Each individual has room to
display its full perfection. The color gathers,
softly flushing from the snow white at one end,
through all rose, pink, cherry, and crimson shades,
to the note of darkest red; the long stems of tender green showing through the clear glass, the
radiant tempered gold of each flower illuminating
the whole. Here and there a few leaves, stalks,
and buds (if I can bring my mind to the cutting
of these last) are sparingly interspersed at the
back. The effect of this arrangement is perfectly
beautiful. It is simply indescribable, and I have
seen people stand before it mute with delight. It
is like the rose of dawn.

To the left of this altar of flowers is a little
table, upon which a picture stands and leans
against the wall at the back. In the picture two
Tea Roses long since faded live yet in their exquisite hues, never indeed to die. Before this I
keep always a few of the fairest flowers, and call
this table the shrine. Sometimes it is a spray of

Madonna Lilies in a long white vase of ground glass, or beneath the picture in a jar of yellow glass floats a saffron-tinted Water Lily, the Chromatella, or a tall sapphire glass holds deep blue Larkspurs of the same shade, or in a red Bohemian glass vase are a few carmine Sweet Peas, another harmony of color, or a charming dull red Japanese jar holds a few Nasturtiums that exactly repeat its hues. The lovely combinations and contrasts of flowers and vases are simply endless.

On another small table below the "altar" are pink Water Lilies in pink glasses and white ones in white glasses ; a low basket of amber glass is filled with the pale turquoise of Forget-me-nots, the glass is iridescent and gleams with changing reflections, taking tints from every color near it. Sweet Peas are everywhere about and fill the air with fragrance ; orange and yellow Iceland Poppies are in tall vases of English glass of light green. There is a large, low bowl, celadon-tinted, and decorated with the boughs and fruit of the Olive on the gray - green background. This is filled with magnificent Jacqueminot Roses, so large, so deep in color as to fully merit the word. Sometimes they are mixed with pink Gabrielle de Luizets and old-fashioned Damask Roses, and the bowl is set where the light falls just as it should to give the splendor of the flowers its full effect. In the centre of a round table under one of the chandeliers is a flaring Venice glass as pure as a drop of dew and of a quaintly lovely shape; on the crystal water therein lies a single white Water Lily, fragrant snow and gold. By itself is a low vase shaped like a Magnolia flower, with petals of light yellow deepening in color at the bottom, where its calyx of olive-green leaves clasps the flower. This has looking over its edge a few pale yellow Nasturtiums of the Asa Gray variety, the lightest of all. With these, one or two of a richer yellow (Dunnett's Orange), the flowers repeating the tones of the vase, and with them harmoniously blending. A large pearly shell of the whelk tribe was given me years ago. I did not know what to do with it. I do not like flowers in shells as a rule, and I think the shells are best on the beach where they belong, but I was fond of the giver, so I sought some way of utilizing the gift. In itself it was beautiful, a mass of glimmering rainbows. I bored three holes in its edge and suspended it from one of the severely simple chandeliers with almost invisible wires. I keep it filled with water and in it arrange sometimes clusters of monthly Honeysuckle sparingly; the hues of the flowers and the shell mingle and blend divinely. I get the same effect with Hydrangea flowers, tints and tones all melt together; so also with the most delicate Sweet Peas, white, rose, and lilac; with these I take some lengths of the blossoming Wild Cucumber vine with its light clusters of white flowers, or the white Clematis, the kind called " Traveler's Joy," and weave it lightly about the shell, letting it creep over one side and, running up the wires, entirely conceal them; then it is like a heavenly apparition afloat in mid air. Sometimes the tender mauve and soft rose and delicate blues of the exquisite little

Rose Campion, or Rose of Heaven, with its grassy foliage, swing in this rainbow shell, making another harmony of hues.

Sometimes it is draped with wild Morning-glory vines which are gathered with their buds at evening; their long wiry stems I coil in the water, and arrange the graceful lengths of leaves and buds carefully, letting a few droop over the edge and twine together beneath the shell, and some run up to the chandelier and conceal the wires. The long smooth buds, yellow-white like ivory, deepen to a touch of bright rose at the tips close folded. In the morning all the buds open into fair trumpets of sea-shell pink, turning to every point of the compass, an exquisite sight to see. By changing the water daily these vines last a week, fresh buds maturing and blossoming every morning.

Near my own seat in a sofa corner at one of the south windows stands yet another small table, covered with a snow-white linen cloth embroidered in silk as white and lustrous as silver. On this are gathered every day all the rarest and loveliest flowers as they blossom, that I may touch them, dwell on them, breathe their delightful fragrance and adore them. Here are kept the daintiest and most delicate of the vases which may best set off the flowers' loveliness, — the smallest of the collection, for the table is only large enough to hold a few. There is one slender small tumbler of colorless glass, from the upper edge of which a crimson stain is diffused half way down its crystal length. In this I keep one glowing

crimson Burgundy Rose, or an opening Jacqueminot bud; the effect is as if the color of the
rose ran down and dyed the glass crimson. It
is so beautiful an effect one never wearies of it.
There is a little jar of Venice glass, the kind
which Browning describes in " The Flight of the
Duchess," —

> " With long white threads distinct inside,
> Like the lake-flower's fibrous roots that dangle
> Loose such a length and never tangle."

This is charming with a few rich Pinks of different shades. Another Venice glass is irregu-
larly bottle-shaped, bluish white with cool sea-
green reflections at the bottom, very delicate, like
an aqua-marine. It is lightly sprinkled with gold
dust throughout its whole length; toward the top
the slender neck takes on a soft touch of pink
which meets and mingles with the Bon Silene or
La France Rose I always keep in it. Another
Venice glass still is a wonder of iridescent blues,
lavenders, gray, and gold, all through, with a faint
hint of elusive green. A spray of heaven-blue
Larkspur dashed with rose is delicious in this
slender shape, with its marvelous tints melting
into the blue and pink of the fairy flowers.

A little glass of crystal girdled with gold holds
pale blue Forget-me-nots; sometimes it is rich
with orange and yellow Erysimum flowers. In
a tall Venetian vase of amber a Lilium auratum
is superb. A low jar of opaque rose-pink, lost at
the bottom in milky whiteness, is refreshing with
an old-fashioned Damask Rose matching its color

exactly. This is also exquisite with one pink Water Lily. The pink variety of the Rose Campion is enchanting in this low jar. A tall shaft of ruby glass is radiant with Poppies of every shade of rose and lightest scarlet, with the silvery green of a few oats among them. A slender purple glass is fine with different shades of purple and lilac Sweet Peas, or one or two purple Poppies, or an Aster or two of just its color, but there is one long gold-speckled Bohemian glass of rich green which is simply perfect for any flower that blows, and perfect under any circumstances. A half dozen Iceland Poppies, white, yellow, orange, in a little Japanese porcelain bottle, always stand on this beautiful table, the few flecks of color on the bottle repeating their tints. I never could tell half the lovely combinations that glow on this table all summer long.

By the wide western window a large vase of clear white glass, nearly three feet high, stands full of spears of timothy grass taller than the vase, the tallest I can find, springing stately and high, their heavy green tops bending the fine strong stems just enough for consummate grace. These are mixed with lighter branching grasses, and down among the grass stalks are thrust the slender stalks of tall Poppies of every conceivable shade of red ; the whole is a great sheaf of splendor reaching higher than the top of the window. This is really imposing ; it takes the eye with delight.

All summer long within this pleasant room the flowers hold carnival in every possible combina-

tion of beauty.   All summer long it is kept fresh
and radiant with their loveliness, — a wonder of
bloom, color, and fragrance.   Year after year a
long procession of charming people come and go
within its doors, and the flowers that glow for
their delight seem to listen with them to the music that stirs each blossom upon its stem.   Often
have I watched the great red Poppies drop their
fiery petals wavering solemnly to the floor, stricken
with arrows of melodious sound from the matchless violin answering to the touch of a master, or
to the storm of rich vibrations from the piano.
What heavenly music has resounded from those
walls, what mornings and evenings of pleasant-
ness have flown by in that room!   How many
people who have been happy there have gone
out of it and of the world forever!   Yet still the
summers come, the flowers bloom, are gathered
and adored, not without wistful thought of the
eyes that will see them no more.   Still in the
sweet tranquil mornings at the piano one sits
playing, also with a master's touch, and strains of
Schubert, Mozart, Schumann, Chopin, Rubin-
stein, Beethoven, and many others, soothe and
enchant the air.   The wild bird's song that breaks
from without into the sonata makes no discord.
Open doors and windows lead out on the vine-
wreathed veranda, with the garden beyond steeped
in sunshine, a sea of exquisite color swaying in
the light air.   Poppies blowing scarlet in the
wind, or delicately flushing in softest rose or
clearest red, or shining white where the Bride
stands tall and fair, like a queen among them all.

A thousand varied hues amid the play of fluttering leaves: Marigolds ablaze in vivid flame; purple Pansies, — a myriad flowers, white, pink, blue, carmine, lavender, in waves of sweet color and perfume to the garden fence, where stand the sentinel Sunflowers and Hollyhocks, gorgeously arrayed and bending gently to the breeze; Sunflowers with broad faces that seem to reflect the glory of the day; the Hollyhocks, tall spikes of pale and deep pink, white, scarlet, yellow, maroon, and many hues. Over the sweet sea of flowers the butterflies go wavering on airy wings of white and gold, the bees hum in the Hollyhocks, and the humming-birds glitter like jewels in the sun; but whether these their winged lovers go or come, the flowers do not care, they live their happy lives and rejoice, intent only on fulfilling Heaven's will, to grow and to blossom in the utmost perfection possible to them. Climbing the trellis, the monthly Honeysuckle holds its clusters high against the pure sunlit sky, glowing in beauty beyond any words of mine to tell. Charming people sit within the pleasant room among its flowers, listening to the delicious music; others are grouped without in the sun-flecked shadow of the green vines, where the cool air ripples lightly in the leaves; lovely women in colors that seem to have copied the flowers in the garden, and all steeped in sweet dreams and fugitive fancies as delicate as the perfumes that drift in soft waves from the blossoms below. Beyond the garden the green grassy spaces sloping to the sea are rich with blossoming thickets of wild Roses, among

the bleached white ledges, blushing fair to see,
and the ocean beyond shimmers and sparkles
beneath the touch of the warm south wind.

Enchanting days, and evenings still more so, if
that were possible! With the music still thrilling within the lighted room where the flowers
glow under the lamplight, while floods of moonlight make more mystic the charmed night without. The thick curtain of the green vine that
drapes the piazza is hung over its whole surface
with the long drooping clusters of its starry flowers that lose all their sweetness upon the air,
and show from the garden beneath like an immense airy veil of delicate white lace in the moonlight, — a wonderful white glory. Through the
windows cut in this living curtain of leaves and
flowers we look out over the sea beneath the
moon — is anything more mysteriously beautiful?
— on glimmering waves and shadowy sails and
rocks dim in broken light and shade; on the
garden with all its flowers so full of color that
even in the moonlight their hues are visibly glowing. The fair creatures stand still, unstirred by
any wandering airs, the Lilies gleam, and the
white stars of the Nicotiana, the white Poppies,
the white Asters that just begin to bloom, and
the tall milky clusters of the Phlox: nothing disturbs their slumber save perhaps the wheeling of
the rosy-winged Sphinx moth that flutters like
the spirit of the night above them as they dream.

HE garden suffers from the long drought in this last week of July, though I water it faithfully. The sun burns so hot that the earth dries again in an hour, after the most thorough drenching I can give it. The patient flowers seem to be standing in hot ashes, with the air full of fire above them. The cool breeze from the sea flutters their drooping petals, but does not refresh them in the blazing noon. Outside the garden on the island slopes the baked turf cracks away from the heated ledges of rock, and all the pretty growths of Sorrel and Eyebright, Grasses and Crowfoot, Potentilla and Lion's-tongue, are crisp and dead. All things begin again to pine and suffer for the healing touch of the rain.

Toward noon on this last day of the month the air darkens, and around the circle of the horizon the latent thunder mutters low. Light puffs of wind eddy round the garden, and whirl aloft the weary Poppy petals high in air, till they wheel like birds about the chimney-tops. Then all is quiet once more. In the rich, hot sky the clouds

pile themselves slowly, superb white heights of
thunder-heads warmed with a brassy glow that
deepens to rose in their clefts toward the sun.
These clouds grow and grow, showing like Alpine
summits amid the shadowy heaps of looser vapor;
all the great vault of heaven gathers darkness;
soon the cloudy heights, melting, are suffused
in each other, losing shape and form and color.
Then over the coast-line the sky turns a hard
gray-green, against which rises with solemn movement and awful deliberation an arch of leaden
vapor spanning the heavens from southwest to
northeast, livid, threatening, its outer edges
shaped like the curved rim of a mushroom,
gathering swiftness as it rises, while the water
beneath is black as hate, and the thunder rolls
peal upon peal, as faster and faster the wild arch
moves upward into tremendous heights above our
heads.   The whole sky is dark with threatening
purple.   Death and destruction seem ready to
emerge from beneath that flying arch of which
the livid fringes stream like gray flame as the
wind rends its fierce and awful edge.   Under it
afar on the black level water a single sail gleams
chalk-white in the gloom, a sail that even as we
look is furled away from our sight, that the frail
craft which bears it may ride out the gale under
bare poles, or drive before it to some haven of
safety.   Earth seems to hold her breath before
the expected fury.   Lightning scores the sky from
zenith to horizon, and across from north to south
"a fierce, vindictive scribble of fire" writes its
blinding way, and the awesome silence is broken

by the cracking thunder that follows every flash. A moment more, and a few drops like bullets strike us; then the torn arch flies over in tattered rags, a monstrous apparition lost in darkness; then the wind tears the black sea into white rage and roars and screams and shouts with triumph, — the floods and the hurricane have it all their own way. Continually the tempest is shot through with the leaping lightning and crashing thunder, like steady cannonading, echoing and reëchoing, roaring through the vast empty spaces of the heavens. In pauses of the tumult a strange light is fitful over sea and rocks, then the tempest begins afresh as if it had taken breath and gained new strength. One's whole heart rises responding to the glory and the beauty of the storm, and is grateful for the delicious refreshment of the rain. Every leaf rejoices in the life-giving drops. Through the dense sparkling rain-curtain the lightning blazes now in crimson and in purple sheets of flame. Oh, but the wind is wild! Spare my treasures, oh, do not slay utterly my beautiful, beloved flowers! The tall stalks bend and strain, the Larkspurs bow. I hold my breath while the danger lasts, thinking only of the wind's power to harm the garden; for the leaping lightning and the crashing thunder I love, but the gale fills me with dread for my flowers defenseless. Still down pour the refreshing floods; everything is drenched: where are the humming-birds? The boats toss madly on the moorings, the sea breaks wildly on the shore, the world is drowned and gone, there is nothing but tempest and tumult and rush and roar of wind and rain.

The long trailing sprays of the Echinocystus vine stretch and strain like pennons flying out in the blast, the Wistaria tosses its feathery plumes over the arch above the door. Alas, for my bank of tall Poppies and blue Cornflowers and yellow Chrysanthemums outside! The Poppies are laid low, never to rise again, but the others will gather themselves together by and by, and the many-colored fires of Nasturtiums will clothe the slope with new beauty presently. The storm is sweeping past, already the rain diminishes, the lightning pales, the thunder retreats till leagues and leagues away we hear it "moaning and calling out of other lands." The clouds break away and show in the west glimpses of pure, melting blue, the sun bursts forth, paints a rainbow in the east upon the flying fragments of the storm, and pours a flood of glory over the drowned earth; the pelted flowers take heart and breathe again, every leaf shines, dripping with moisture; the grassy slopes laugh in sweet color; the sea calms itself to vast tranquillity and answers back the touch of the sun with a million glittering smiles.

Though the outside bank of flowers is wrecked and the tall Poppies prone upon the ground, those inside the garden are safe because I took the precaution to run two rows of wire netting up and down through the beds for their support. So, when the winds are cruelly violent, the tall, brittle stalks lean against this light but strong bulwark and are unhurt.

After the storm, in the clear, beautiful morning, before sunrise I went as usual into the garden to gather my flowers. To and fro, up and down over the ruined bank I passed; the wind blew cool and keen from the west, though the sky was smiling. The storm had beaten the flowers flat all over the slope; in scarlet and white and blue and pink and purple and orange bloom they were prostrate everywhere, leaves, stalks, blossoms, and all tangled and matted in an inextricable confusion. Swiftly I made my way through it, finding a foothold here and there, and stooping for every freshly unfolded cup or star or bell whose bud the tempest had spared. As I neared the little western gate with my hands full of blossoms to enter the garden on my way to the house, I was stopped still as a statue before a most pathetic sight. There, straight across the way, a tall Poppy plant lay prone upon the ground, and clinging to the stem of one of its green seed-pods sat my precious pet humming-bird, the dearest of the flock that haunt the garden, the tamest of them all. His eyes were tightly closed, his tiny claws clasped the stem automatically, he had no feeling, he was rigid with cold. The chill dew loaded the gray-green Poppy leaves, the keen wind blew sharply over him, — he is dead, I thought with a pang, as I shifted my flowers in a glowing heap to my left arm, and clasped the frozen little body in the palm of my right hand. It was difficult to disengage his slender wiry claws from their close grip on the chilly stalk, but he never moved or showed a sign of life as I took

him off. I held him most tenderly in my closed
hand, very careful not to crush or even press his
tiny perishing body, and breathed into the shut
hollow of my palm upon him with a warm and
loving breath. I was so very busy, there were so
many things to be done that morning, I could not
stop to sit down and nurse him back to life. But
I held him safe, and as I went up and down the
garden paths gathering the rest of my flowers, I
breathed every moment into my hand upon him.
Ten, fifteen, twenty minutes passed; he made no
sign of life. Alas, I thought, he is truly dead;
when all at once I felt the least little thrill pass
through the still, cold form, an answering thrill
of joy ran through me in response, and more
softly, closely, tenderly yet I sent my warm breath
to the tiny creature as I still went on with my
work. In a few minutes more I began to feel
the smallest fluttering pulse of life throbbing
faintly within him; in yet a few moments more
he stirred and stretched his wings, comforting
himself in the genial heat. When at last I felt
him all alive, I took a small shallow basket of
yellow straw, very small and light, and in it put
a tuft of soft cotton wool, filled a tiny glass cup
with sugar and water, honey-thick, placed it in the
basket by the cotton, then gently laid the wee bird
on the warm fluff. His eyes were still closed,
but he moved his head slowly from side to side.
The sun had risen and was pouring floods of light
and heat into the garden. I carried the basket
out into the corner where the heavenly blue Larkspurs stood behind the snow-whiteness of the full

blossoming Lilies, and among the azure spikes I
hung the pretty cradle where the sunbeams lay
hottest and brightest on the flowers. The wind,
grown balmy and mild, rocked the tall flower-
spikes gently, the basket swayed with them, and
the heat was so reviving that the dear little creature presently opened his eyes and quietly looked
about him. At that my heart rejoiced. It was
delightful to watch his slow return to his old self
as I still went on with my work, looking continually toward him to see how he was getting on.
The ardent sunbeams sent fresh life through him;
suddenly he rose, an emerald spark, into the air,
and quivered among the blue flowers, diving deep
into each winged blossom for his breakfast of
honey.

All day and every day he haunts the garden,
and when tired rests contentedly on the small twig
of a dry pea-stick near the Larkspurs. The rosy
Peas blossom about him, the Hollyhock flowers
unfold in glowing pink with lace-like edges of
white; the bees hum there all day in and out of
the many flowers; the butterflies hover and waver
and wheel. When one comes too near him, up
starts my beauty and chases him away on burnished wings, away beyond the garden's bounds,
and returns to occupy his perch in triumph, — the
dry twig he has taken for his home the whole
sweet summer long. Other humming-birds haunt
the place, but he belongs there; they go and come,
but he keeps to his perch and his Larkspurs faithfully. He is so tame he never stirs from his twig
for anybody, no matter how near a person may

come ; he alights on my arms and hands and hair unafraid; he rifles the flowers I hold, when I am gathering them, and I sometimes think he is the very most charming thing in the garden. The jealous bees and the butterflies follow the flowers I carry also, sometimes all the way into the house. The other day, as I sat in the piazza which the vines shade with their broad green leaves and sweet white flowers climbing up to the eaves and over the roof, I saw the humming-birds hovering over the whole expanse of green, to and fro, and discovered that they were picking off and devouring the large transparent aphides scattered, I am happy to say but sparingly, over its surface, every little gnat and midge they snapped up with avidity. I had fancied they lived on honey, but they appeared to like the insects quite as well.

In the sweet silence before sunrise, standing in the garden I watch the large round shield of the full moon slowly fading in the west from copper to brass and then to whitest silver, throwing across a sea of glass its long, still reflection, while the deep, pure sky takes on a rosy warmth of color from the approaching sun. Soon an insufferable glory burns on the edge of the eastern horizon; up rolls the great round red orb and sets the dew twinkling and sparkling in a thousand rainbows, sending its first rejoicing rays over the wide face of the world. When in these fresh mornings I go into my garden before any one is awake, I go for the time being into perfect happiness. In this hour divinely fresh and still, the fair face of every flower salutes me with a silent joy that fills me

with infinite content; each gives me its color, its grace, its perfume, and enriches me with the consummation of its beauty. All the cares, perplexities, and griefs of existence, all the burdens of life slip from my shoulders and leave me with the heart of a little child that asks nothing beyond its present moment of innocent bliss. These myriad beaming faces turned to mine seem to look at me with blessing eyes. I feel the personality of each flower, and I find myself greeting them as if they were human. "Good-morning, beloved friends! Are all things well with you? And are you tranquil and bright? and are you happy and beautiful?" They stand in their peace and purity and lift themselves to my adoring gaze as if they knew my worship, — so calm, so sweet, so delicately radiant, I lose myself in the tranquillity of their happiness. They seem like sentient beings, as if they knew me and loved me, not indeed as I love them, but with almost a reliance on my sympathy and care, and a pleasure in my delight in them. I please myself with the thought that if anything goes wrong with them, if a vine or tender stalk droops for lack of support, or if some insect is working them woe, or threat of harm comes to them from any quarter, they say to each other, "Patience! She will be coming soon, she will see our trouble, she will succor us, and all will again be well."

The summer life in the garden of the winged things of the air is most charming, — the wonderful creatures that have escaped, as it were, from the earth. The life that crawls and creeps and devours and destroys, in the forms of slug and cutworm and all hideous shapes, is utterly forgotten as we watch these ethereal beings, fluttering, quivering, darting, dancing, wavering, wheeling, rejoicing aloft in merry flight.   The Larkspur spikes bend with the weight of the booming bees, the whole blossoming space is alive with many-colored butterflies like floating flowers, and the humming-birds are a perpetual pleasure.   They are astir even before sunrise, when the air is yet chill with the breath of the retreating night, — there they are, vibrating with their soft humming over the Larkspur blossoms which are themselves like exquisite azure birds all poised for flight, or diving deep into the fragrant trumpets of the Honeysuckle, everywhere flashing in emerald and ruby as the sun's first beams strike them, like the living jewels they are.   Their fearlessness is something amazing.   I never shall forget the surprise of joy that filled me when for the first time one alighted on my sleeve and rested, as much at home as if I were a stick or a harmless twig ! Sparrows and nuthatches had often alighted on my head as I stood musing over my flowers, perfectly still, but to have this tiny spark of brilliant life come to anchor, as it were, on anything so earthly as my arm was indeed a nine days' wonder ! Now it has grown to be an old story, but it is never any less delightful.

August 18th. This morning the garden was so dry again when I sought it at sunrise, in spite of the heavy dew, that I took the hose and turned on the water, showering the whole place most

thoroughly. When I had done the drops clung
thickly to everything, to the sprays of Sweet Peas
especially, the rough surface of their leaves
and stalks catching and holding the water more
tenaciously than the smoother foliage; they were
begemmed, as it were, with so many sparkling
spheres of light. The tamest, dearest humming-
bird, whose home is in the Larkspurs, was greatly
excited by this unexpected and refreshing shower,
and whirred about me, uttering continually his
one fine, sweet, keen note. When my rain-storm
ceased he flew to the Sweet Peas close to his
azure bower, and sitting on a green spray already
bent with the weight of the clear drops, proceeded
to take his morning bath with the most cheerful
enjoyment. He fluttered his tiny wings and
ducked his head and wagged his tail and drenched
himself completely; his feathers were so soaking
wet that his little body looked no bigger than a
bumble-bee; then he flew up and lighted on the
tallest pea-stick that reached over the fence
among the Larkspurs: there sitting on his favorite
twig he rapidly preened his feathers, shook himself, spread his wings and tail and combed them
with his slender beak and dried them in the
broad, bright beams that poured across the garden from the low sun. With claws and beak he
smoothed and arranged his dainty raiment, perfectly regardless of me, his ardent admirer, standing near enough to touch him with my finger.
Then he fluttered in and out among the flowers,
dipping into every dewy chalice and feasting on
his fragrant honey.

I wonder, as I muse over the charms of these most minute of feathered creatures, how it is possible for their tiny wings to bear them over the miles of restless and perilous brine, to find this rock with its nest of flowers! Do they surmise the hospitality that awaits them at the end of their long journey as they steer their dangerous way across the wastes of the salt sea on those small, weak, quivering pinions? Have they some subtle inkling of the tender welcome that awaits them here? Do they guess how they will be admired and adored? I have filled a small glass mug with sugar and water thick as honey, and fastened it in a crotch of the pea-sticks for them to feed upon; the bees throng to it, the ants have found it, and I hope the humming-birds will feast there too. One morning lately, as I was busy in the garden, a little creature brushed by me so close I thought it was a bee; turning to look at it, I was sure it was a humming-bird, but such an atom! Its like I had never imagined. I watched it, fascinated, as it flew here, there, and everywhere, whirring just like a humming-bird, crazy over the annual Larkspurs. A greenish golden sheen was reflected from the head and back, the very color of the little bird, and it had a small, short tail, with a band of white round its body, which seemed feathered, as also its mottled breast. Its bright black eyes were like the bird's, and it hummed with its wings in precisely the same way. Its beak was short, and as it went from flower to flower, probing for honey, I was perfectly sure it was a new variety of humming-bird, the most minute that was ever created. I watched it with breathless interest, completely puzzled by it. Perfectly tame, it flew all about me and investigated the flowers in my hand. Suddenly I discovered that it had three pairs of legs! No bird, I said, ever had more than one, and then I was satisfied that it must be the most marvelous moth in the world. It was so happy and beautiful, flying about so confidingly in the bright sunshine within reach of my hand! But I knew of some one to whom it would be a treasure, so I threw a light veil over, caught it, and sent it softly to sleep forever with some chloroform. It was *Ællopos Titan*, very rare, and found in the tropics.

The dazzling white Lilies blossoming now, bright as silvery snow below the Larkspurs, are taller than they by several feet. I wish I could in any words paint the hues of these splendid Delphiniums ; such shades of melting blue, some light, others dark, some like the summer heaven, and dashed across their pale azure wings with delicious rose. Now is the garden at high tide of beauty. Sweet Peas are brilliant in all their vivid tints; they are doing bravely, spite of the drought, because their roots are so well shaded. They bloom so plenteously that they can hardly be gathered, though they are cut daily. The Rose Campion bed is a lake of delicate colors with its border of scarlet Flax. Poppies of every tint are blazing; the Hollyhocks are splendid, with their comrades the Sunflowers; every day the single Dahlias surprise me with new and unexpected flowers ; the Tea Rose bed is a perpetual delight

and astonishment; the purple Zanzibar Lily is
blossoming in its tub and never is without its
wonderful cup afloat; the Lotus sends up strong,
long-stemmed leaves aloft, and keeps me eagerly
looking for its promised flower of radiant pink, —
its leaves are a marvel with their mystic markings
held so high above the water. The Honeysuckles
are breathing out all their sweetness on the air;
the Pinks are out in spicy bloom; the Mountain
Fringe drapes the doorway with cloudy green
and pale rose-color. Constellations of Marigolds
and Artemisias and Coreopsis, whole solar sys-
tems of fiery suns and stars, blossom all over the
place, and in partly shaded corners large fragrant
stars of Nicotiana shine also when twilight falls.
The Japanese Sunflowers make every spot gay
where they unfold; they are hardy; when once
they fairly get a foothold in the garden, they will
not be dislodged, and I for one would never wish
to dislodge them, though they spread and grow
and multiply rapidly, and take much space if left
to go on undisturbed. They have an indescribable golden atmosphere about them, because, I sup-
pose, of their cup-like shape; they never stretch
their petals out flat like other Sunflowers. They
have a small brown central disk, and their "ray-
like florets" are of deep yellow, curved more in-
ward than outward. The Artemisias are in one
shade of full, rich gold, in shape like a common
field Daisy; the Marigolds are in every shade of
yellow, orange, and flame, effulgent, — some with
centres of velvet brown, some with peacock green,
some all gold, with exquisite gradations of color

through all their rays. "Ardent Marigolds!" sang John Keats. Ardent indeed they are, with fervors of color that glow like the beams of day.

The dark crimson Jacqueminot Roses are almost gone, but almost every other flower is at its best, the whole garden in blossom at once. Dearly I love to sit in the sun upon the doorstep with a blossom in my hand and meditate upon its details, the lavish elaboration of its loveliness, to study every peculiar characteristic of each, and wonder and rejoice in its miraculous existence, a feast more delicate and satisfying than the honey the birds and bees and butterflies gather from its heart. Over my head the Coboea vine droops its large green and purple bells, with many another flower beside. The Tropæolum Lucifer thronging up the trellis on either hand truly merits the name of Light-bearer; its scarlet velvet blooms have almost an illuminating quality. I hold a flower of the pretty Love-in-a-mist, the quaint Nigella, and scan its charming face. It blossoms late and long, and is a flower of most distinguished beauty. It is star-shaped, in tints of white, blue, and purple, with full rich stamens and anthers of warmer red-purple, the petals on the back delicately veined in each variety with fine lines of faint green. The rich cluster of stamens is surrounded at the base by eight smaller inner petals in different tints, so wonderful in detail, so ornate in decoration as to be simply indescribable. Each large outer petal is curved and cup-shaped, yet each has its finishing point which makes the blossom starry, and these eight inner petals radiate from the centre within, above the larger ones. The foliage whence it gets its old-time name, Love-in-a-mist, is like a soft green vapor, and in the double varieties, the white especially, runs up and mixes itself with the petals. The single varieties are much the finest. They have a faint perfume of anise, and they are among the quaintest and most interesting flowers I know.

I love to pore over every blossom that unfolds in the garden, no matter what it may be, to study it and learn it by heart as far as a poor mortal may. If one but gazes closely into a tiny flower of the pale blue Forget-me-not, what a chapter of loveliness is there! One sees at a glance the sweet color of the starry, compact cluster, and perhaps will notice that the delicate buds in their cherishing calyx are several shades of rose and lilac before they unclose, but unless one studies it closely, how shall one know that in most cases the *himmel-blau* petals are distinctly heart-shaped, that round its golden centre it wears a necklace of pearls, or so they seem, till on looking closer one discovers that the effect is made by the fluting of the whitened folds of each petal at the base; it looks precisely as if it wore a string of polished beads. The tiny spot of darkness within its inmost yellow ring holds five stamens, with dusty anthers of paler yellow (also heart-shaped when the flower first unfolds) in a close circle round the pistil of pale green. Unless the eyes are young and keen a microscope only will tell this; but it is one of the wisest things in the world to carry in one's pocket a little magnifying

glass, for this opens so many unknown gates into
the wonders and splendors of Creation. There
is such wealth of ornament, such marvelous sub-
tile thought spent on the smallest blossom! The
" sweet and cunning hand of Nature " is so lavish
of its work, and it is all so happy, the joy is so
inexhaustible, the refreshment to the human soul
so heavenly!

The fragrant fringes of the Mignonette, how
surprising and curiously beautiful they are under
the little pocket microscope! What elaboration
of detail, what tempered harmonies of color, what
marvels of construction! I reach my hand for a
blossom of Coreopsis Coronata some one has let
fall on the step, — what a refulgent flower! There
is something Spanish about its aspect always to
me. There are eight yellow velvet petals deeply
toothed at the edges, and rich embroideries in
red about the warmer yellow of the centre. Gorgeous it is, and so is its relative, Coreopsis Drummondii, and both have a double row of sepals, the
row nearest the corolla brown and thin and light,
the outer one much coarser and bright green.
The centre of the Drummondii is more like the
wild Rudbeckia, with markings not so ornate as
the Coronata, but in a mass, and of a brighter,
clearer red. All this family of flowers, Lanceolata, Golden Banner, the deep scarlet and maroon
varieties, are superb and most decorative.

It is a great temptation to linger over the loveliness of every flower that unfolds, but I spare
my patient readers, and leave them to pursue
these fascinating researches for themselves.

I have had reward enough for all my care of the Water Lilies (even though they had put forth only leaves, but they have blossomed well) in the delight of the birds over the tubs of clear water on which the mottled leaves are floating.   So many charming creatures pause at them to drink, and the song-sparrows bathe there daily.   Enchanting it is to watch their pretty ways as they hop from the tub's edge upon a Lily-pad which yields beneath their weight and lets them gently down, but out of this they always flit and take their own way about it, dipping and splashing bravely till they are thoroughly drenched, then preening and drying themselves as they sit upon the brim, and singing their song of sweet content when all is done.

September 23d.   Now are the crickets loud in the grass and the Hawkweed waves in pale yellow all over the island, the autumn Dandelion, starry on its long and slender stem.   But still the garden glows, and still autumn

> " Sets budding more
> And still more later flowers for the bees,
> Until they think warm days will never cease,
> For summer has o'er brimmed their clammy cells."

Where the Hollyhocks earliest to blossom stand bereft of all save their thick-growing, full, round seed vessels, the late Morning - glories have wreathed and twined themselves and hung the stems with white and rose and heaven-blue bells, and the later blooming stalks are rich with fresh flowers.   Still the Sweet Peas blossom as if their thick ranks were ready to fly away with myriad wings of delicious pink, blue, purple, red, and white. Poppies yet bloom, Rose Campions at their brightest, hemmed in with the Scarlet Flax, and the stars and suns of Marigolds blaze with a matchless glory. Single Dahlias are sumptuous in every color, and in their prime. One Coreopsis Golden Banner is a sight to see, like a great gold mountain heaped in the middle of the garden. Many kinds of Helianthus make splendid the little inclosure; Love-in-a-mist puts out flower after flower of mystic charm; the Asters bloom in profusion of exquisite colors,—the Comet variety, which I think is most lovely of all. The white Stocks are dazzling in their purity, and so fragrant! Nasturtiums run riot, of course, and light up every corner; the Phloxes glow; the Mourning Brides are fine in their sumptuous black-red velvet; Verbenas are brilliant; Tea Roses blossoming yet; the Giant Spider flower, *Cloeme pungens*, rises all over the garden in rosy purple clouds. Mignonette is lavish of rich spikes of bloom, and the Pansies never so splendid; immense smooth, perfect flowers of every color, they never put forth such in the summer heats. Picotee pinks are bright and sweet, but the poor little Margarets suffered too much with the venomous carnation worm, spite of my daily care, and are only just now sending up their buds. I shall take them up and keep them safe in the house over the winter. In a corner the deep blue Plumbago Lady Larpent blooms finely, the Foxgloves are strong and tall, though they will not blossom

till another year; but the whole garden is a mass
of bloom and fragance, still haunted by birds,
bees, butterflies, and dragonflies; the humming-
birds are gone, I know not whither, not to return
this year. The withering vines are alive with
many little creepers and warblers and flycatchers;
indeed, the island is full of distinguished bird-
strangers on their way south. Scores of golden
woodpeckers, or flickers, or yellow-hammers (they
have dozens of striking names) are here, and just
now two great ospreys perch on the vane above
the highest ridge-pole, and soar and perch again,
uttering strange, harsh cries. This morning a
large flock of wild geese flew over toward the
south, so low we could see the colors and the
markings of their plumage. The familiar curlews
call sweetly as in spring. Outside the garden
this tranquil morning the soft green turf that
slopes smoothly to the sea in front is shaggy with
the thick dew from which the yet low sun strikes
a thousand broken rainbows. The clumps of
wild Roses glow with their red haws in the full
light; the Elder bushes are laden with clusters of
purple berries; Goldenrod and wild Asters bloom,
and a touch of fire begins to light up the Huckle-
berry bushes, "Autumn laying here and there a
fiery finger on the leaves." The gray rocks show
so fair in the changing lights, and all the dear
island with its sights and sounds is set in the
pale light summer-blue of a smiling sea as if it
were June, with hardly a wave to break its happy
calm. Round the horizon a band of haze, the
same ashes-of-roses color as that which makes

lovely the skies of May, holds the fair world in a light embrace for this one day; a few white clouds are losing themselves in the pure blue above; a few sails gleam afar. Though the tide is full, it makes no murmur; I hear only the drowsy bees in the Hollyhocks, the young fledgling song-sparrows trying their voices, learning the sweet song their parents are pouring at intervals on the quiet air, and the chirp and twitter of other birds, birds of passage, with finch and thrush, nuthatch and late robin, the whistle of a whitethroat, the clanking jar of the kingfisher that perches on the mast of the faithful little tug Pinafore (so many years our only link with the mainland in winter), as she lies at her wharf in the upper cove, and shows his handsome blue and gray plumage and white collar glittering in the sun. A fisherman draws his nets in a shining white skiff, but he makes no sound that I can hear. The season is so divinely tranquil and sweet, all things are so beautiful in and about the little isle, from the glittering seal that emerges from the waves to sun himself sometimes on the seaweed-covered rocks, to the smallest flower that blossoms in my garden; from the wonderful jelly-fish that spreads its large diaphanous cup, expanding and contracting as it swims, and colored like a great melting opal in the pale-green, translucent water, to the bright-eyed bats that flitter at dusk when the evening star is sparkling above the rich red of the sunset sky. And that reminds me that all summer a white bat has skittered ghostly with its dark companions, as soon as twilight fell, about the place.

Of a white bat never before have I heard, but all kinds of strange and remarkable creatures find their way here, and I am surprised at nothing.

Once more the weird laughter of the loons comes to my ear, the distance lends it a musical, melancholy sound. From a dangerous ledge off the lighthouse island floats in on the still air the gentle tolling of a warning bell as it swings on its rocking buoy ; it might be tolling for the passing of summer and sweet weather with that persistent, pensive chime.

And so the ripe year wanes. From turfy slopes afar the breeze brings delicious, pungent, spicy odors from the wild Everlasting flowers, and the mushrooms are pearly in the grass. I gather the seed-pods in the garden beds, sharing their bounty with the birds I love so well, for there are enough and to spare for us all. Soon will set in the fitful weather, with fierce gales and sullen skies and frosty air, and it will be time to tuck up safely my Roses and Lilies and the rest for their long winter sleep beneath the snow, where I never forget them, but ever dream of their wakening in happy summers yet to be.